TO JOSHUA

An Hachette UK Company
www.hachette.co.uk

First published in Great Britain in 2019 by Cassell
an imprint of Octopus Publishing Group Ltd
Carmelite House
50 Victoria Embankment
London EC4Y 0DZ
www.octopusbooks.co.uk
www.octopusbooks.com

Distributed in the US by
Hachette Book Group
1290 Avenue of the Americas
4th and 5th Floors
New York, NY 10104

Distributed in Canada by
Canadian Manda Group
664 Annette St.
Toronto, Ontario, Canada M6S 2C8

ISBN 978 1 78840 0 749

A CIP catalogue record for this book is available from the
British Library.

Printed and bound in China

10 9 8 7 6 5 4 3 2 1

For this edition:
Senior Commissioning Editor: Joe Cottington
Assistant Editor: Emily Brickell
Designer: Jack Storey
Senior Production Controller: Allison Gonsalves
Translation: Simon Jones

Original concept: Marçais&Marchand
Editorial direction: Nicolas Marçais
Artistic direction: Philippe Marchand
Editorial: Carole Daprey
Design: Élise Godmuse and Emigreen
Illustration: Thierry Freiberg
Photo Reproduction: Émilie Greenberg

50 YEARS

THE STORY OF
Woodstock live

RELIVE THE MAGIC
ARTIST BY ARTIST.

JULIEN BITOUN
FOREWORD BY
WOODSTOCK CO-FOUNDER MICHAEL LANG

 CASSELL ILLUSTRATED

When we embarked on the road to Woodstock, a major concern of mine was that the message and the music support each other. Three Days of Peace and Music was an invitation to the counterculture of the late 1960s to join in a celebration of our ideals, our music, and our art. It was a moment out of time where our struggles against the status quo, our fears of the draft, our opposition to a war we felt unjust, and our fight for equality and personal freedoms could be shared without the pressures of conservative society and growing violence in the streets.

Music was how we communicated our message, and most of the groups that performed were deeply immersed in our world. Other than new talents, such as Crosby, Stills, Nash & Young, Joe Cocker, Mountain, and Santana—who were chosen based on personal taste—I did the booking with this in mind.

Because Woodstock took place before the advent of cell phones, and with CB radio devices being undependable, the stage was the best vantage point to keep abreast of what was happening in the audience. As a consequence, I spent much of the three days at a command point stage right. This afforded me the great gift of seeing most of the performances that weekend.

At 5:07 p.m. on August 15, 1969, Richie Havens walked on stage with his big Guild acoustic guitar, propped himself up on a tall wooden stool, and the festival was officially ON!

However, at the end of his 40-minute set, I could not let Richie off the stage, because (due to the traffic mess) we did not have another group ready to go. We sent him back for six or seven encores and, when he finally ran out of songs, he just started singing "Freedom." It became an anthem for that incredible weekend.

There were so many incredible sets, but the ones that stand out the most are: Crosby, Stills, Nash & Young (their second show ever); Richie Havens (who set the perfect tone for the weekend); Ravi Shankar; Country Joe McDonald (and the "FISH" cheer); Sly & The Family Stone (who took the entire congregation to church with "I Want to Take You Higher"); Joe Cocker (who blew everyone's mind with "With a Little Help from My Friends"); Janis Joplin; Creedence Clearwater Revival—and, of course, Jimi Hendrix.

Michael Lang
Woodstock co-founder

PROLOGUE

SATURDAY, AUGUST 16, 1969

FRIDAY, AUGUST 15, 1969

SUNDAY, AUGUST 17, 1969

EPILOGUE

Political and Social Context
Monterey Pop Festival
Young Men with Unlimited Capital

PROLOGUE

POLITICAL AND SOCIAL CONTEXT

Vietnam in mind

Woodstock was held when the United States was in a period of turbulence. Political and social unrest had been increasing steadily during the 1960s, and finally found a voice on Max Yasgur's farm.

At the time of Woodstock, the Vietnam War was the most pressing and worrying issue for both the audience and musicians. It was discussed on stage between songs in the hope that the huge crowd might be able to make a difference. It was also mentioned in lyrics, through both direct references and more discreet allusions. The war had been going on since 1955, but Lyndon B. Johnson's assumption of the U.S. presidency in 1963 led to the fighting becoming much more intense and devastating. The draft became a sword of Damocles hanging over the head of most young men. By the time Johnson vacated the Oval Office in January 1969, 30,000 American soldiers had already met their deaths in Vietnam. Nixon won the 1968 election promising that he would bring the war to an end, but the conflict dragged on for another six years until 1975.

MARTIN LUTHER KING JR.
1929—1968

Say it loud

At the same time, numerous citizens' organizations were fighting for their dignity. What was to become the civil rights movement had its roots in the struggle African Americans had against the racist Jim Crow laws in the American South. Racial segregation was still in force, but its absurdity was starting to become ever more obvious to the majority of citizens. This movement crystallized around the March on Washington in 1963, which culminated in Martin Luther King Jr.'s famous "I Have a Dream" speech. Music was already carrying the message of this struggle, thanks to artists who played at these protest marches (Joan Baez and Bob Dylan played at the March on Washington) or composed songs that criticized the poor treatment of African Americans.

The civil rights movement achieved some resounding successes, such as securing voting rights for African Americans in 1965 and the ban on discrimination in the sale or rental of housing in 1968. This was undeniable proof that a determined crowd could change the world, especially with the help of music. In retrospect, the Woodstock poster was relatively diverse for its time, because it featured women (Grace Slick, Joan Baez, and Janis Joplin), African Americans (Sly and Richie Havens), and Chicanos and Cherokees (Carlos Santana, for example).

Yin and Yang

The summer of 1969 was a special moment in American history, defined by two events that would shape the following decades, and that throw light on the state of mind of the festivalgoers.

ONE GIANT LEAP

The first of these two events took place on July 20, when the Apollo 11 lunar module landed on the moon. Buzz Aldrin and Neil Armstrong were the first humans to set foot on the moon, and their first steps were filmed and broadcast on television. Proud Americans, they firmly planted the U.S. flag on the lunar surface. The first country to land humans on the moon, the United States of America had effectively won the technological and scientific race against the U.S.S.R. The message was clear: America could do whatever it wanted, and science had revolutionized the world by redefining the frontiers of what was possible.

MURDER IN THE FAMILY

The second event occurred on August 9, less than a week before the start of the festival. It was the day that Sharon Tate was killed. This 26-year-old woman, wife of the movie director Roman Polanski, was brutally murdered. She was eight months pregnant at the time. The crime itself was shocking, but the identity of the murderer was even more devastating for the country: Charles Manson was the perfect symbol of the hippie dream, turned nightmare. Manson was a singer and songwriter who lived in San Francisco's Haight-Ashbury neighborhood, but he was also the leader of a sect called The Family.

Despite this highly charged atmosphere, the Woodstock festival passed off without any violence. It was almost miraculous given the circumstances and the mood of the country.

Historic Performances Recorded at the

MONTEREY INTERNATIONAL POP FESTIVAL
THE MAMAS & THE PAPAS

MONTEREY
POP FESTIVAL

THE ROCK FESTIVAL

Before Monterey, the concept of the rock festival did not exist. There were the Newport Jazz Festival, the Monterey Jazz Festival, the Newport Folk Festival, and the Big Sur Folk Festival, but these were deaf to the growing presence of rock on the turntables of the younger generation. Indeed, Bob Dylan's electric set at Newport Folk Festival in 1965 had remained in people's minds as an anomaly, almost a provocation. It was not until four visionary organizers took the initiative that rock got its festival at last.

HIGH SPIRITS

The year 1967 saw the Summer of Love. It was the year of the Garden of Eden before the Fall. Of course, civil rights demonstrations were reverberating across college campuses, but cynicism had not yet gained the upper hand over blissful optimism, and drug overdoses had not yet begun to ravage the music scene. Monterey, California, became an opportunity for musicians from all over the country—and the world—to meet, sometimes for the first time, while playing similar kinds of music. Monterey is around a two hours' drive from San Francisco, so the location was perfect for encouraging musicians to stay the whole weekend. Even those who were not performing joined the party, taking advantage of the community spirit that took hold. Notably, Brian Jones was in the audience, although The Rolling Stones were not performing, and he introduced The Jimi Hendrix Experience before their set.

THE LINEUP

(Artists marked with an asterisk also appeared at Woodstock)

FRIDAY, JUNE 16
The Association
The Paupers
Lou Rawls
Beverley
Johnny Rivers
Eric Burdon & The Animals
Simon & Garfunkel

SATURDAY, JUNE 17
Canned Heat *
Big Brother & The Holding Company
Country Joe & The Fish *
Al Kooper
The Butterfield Blues Band *
Quicksilver Messenger Service
Steve Miller Band
The Electric Flag
Moby Grape
Hugh Masekela
The Byrds
Laura Nyro
Jefferson Airplane *
Booker T. & The M.G.'s
Otis Redding

SUNDAY, JUNE 18
Ravi Shankar *
The Blues Project
Big Brother & The Holding Company
The Group With No Name
Buffalo Springfield
The Who *
Grateful Dead *
The Jimi Hendrix Experience *
The Mamas & The Papas

A model for Woodstock

Without Monterey, there probably would have been no Woodstock; Michael Lang's team drew their inspiration largely from what had made the former so successful. Eight artists performed at both festivals—not counting Janis Joplin, who was the vocalist of Big Brother & The Holding Company at Monterey, and Crosby, Stills, Nash & Young, who were still respectively members of The Byrds (Crosby) and Buffalo Springfield (Stills and Young). Chip Monck was in charge of lighting at Monterey, and so he was invited to Woodstock, where he also acted as presenter in between the acts. Unfortunately, Woodstock's organizers did not take their cue from Monterey in regards to the sound system—that of the Californian festival was a technical tour de force, designed specially for the occasion, and groups continued to sing its praises after the festival.

However, any comparison seems unfair, because the most important element of all changed completely between the two events. Monterey was held in front of an audience of 90,000 people, whereas Woodstock attracted almost 500,000 fans.

YOUNG MEN
WITH
UNLIMITED CAPITAL

The story of Woodstock begins with an advertisement placed in *The Wall Street Journal* in 1967. It stated that two "young men with unlimited capital" were seeking projects to finance. The two men in question were John Roberts, 22 years old and heir to a pharmaceutical empire, and Joel Rosenman, 25, who had turned down a contract as an artist with the Columbia record label to devote himself to business.

Among the thousands of responses they received, one project caught their eye. It came from Michael Lang, 24 years old, and Artie Kornfeld, 25 years old. The former ran a head shop in Florida, while the latter was vice president of Capitol Records and, despite his young age, the writer of numerous hit songs. Michael and Artie sensed the importance that the town of Woodstock was gaining in the cultural landscape of the time, when Greenwich Village had lost its luster, and he wanted to set up a recording studio near there.

Eventually, the project evolved into a plan for a rock festival. Artie Kornfeld quit his job at the record label, and the four set up the Woodstock Venture office in Manhattan in January 1969. Then they set to work to find the venue and the groups.

Michael Lang and Artie Kornfeld, deeply engrossed in organizing the Woodstock Music and Art Fair.

A general outcry

Lang and Kornfeld initially envisaged holding the festival where their planned recording studio would have been, in Wallkill, New York. But the local residents quickly got wind of the possible arrival of a hippie festival near their homes, and categorically rejected it. Saugerties, an hour north of Wallkill and much closer to Woodstock, was considered next, but negotiations broke down. Rosenman and Roberts then got on the case, and they found a different venue in Wallkill. There, too, the residents got involved and—surprise, surprise—in July the municipal authority passed a law obliging the organizers of an event for more than 5,000 people to apply for a permit. Naturally, Woodstock Venture was refused this permit, on the pretext that the portable toilets it proposed to install did not comply with regulations. The festival was due to be held in a month's time, but it did not yet have a definitive venue.

Max Yasgur's farm

Lang met Max Yasgur, the owner of a dairy farm in Bethel, through the writer Elliot Tiber. Yasgur agreed to make his land available to the festivalgoers—thus saving Woodstock. What is more, his farm was a bowl of land, which naturally made it possible to see the stage clearly even from a distance. Behind the stage, at the end of the plot of land, the Filippini Pond made a pretty backdrop and an ideal playground for the hippies. Despite protests, the municipal authority granted Woodstock a permit. At that point, the organizers expected to welcome 50,000 people.

Woodstock for 7 dollars

Tickets were priced at 7 dollars per day and 18 dollars for three days. However, the venue had been decided on so late that the organizers decided to prioritize finishing setting up the stage over erecting barriers around the festival site. A huge surge of people arrived and the crowd could not be contained, so the festival became free.

> "A half a million young people can get together and have three days of fun and music and have nothing **but** fun and music, and God bless you for it!"

MAX YASGUR

The dove and her guitar

The Woodstock poster is much more than a mere advertisement for a concert; it has become one of the most powerful and lasting symbols of the hippie generation. However, it was produced in a hurry. Following the change of venue from Wallkill to Bethel, it had to be completely revised, and the artist Arnold Skolnick was contacted on a Thursday and asked to deliver the poster the following Monday morning. So he produced this simple image of a dove (actually a catbird) perched on the neck of a guitar (a perfect depiction of "Peace and Music") by cutting up pieces of paper and making a collage to create the famous design. Originally, the background was to have been blue to symbolize peace; however, red was eventually chosen because the bird already provided the symbolism. Skolnick was paid 15 dollars (the equivalent of about 115 dollars today), and he never received any fees for reproductions of his work.

A

FRIDAY, AUGUST 15, 1969

FROM FRIDAY 5:07 P.M.
TO SATURDAY 1:00 A.M.

The group Sweetwater was supposed to kick things off, but when they should have been on stage, they were still on their way, caught in traffic. So Richie Havens, a New Yorker, stepped in at short notice to deliver the festival's first performance—a moment of communion with the audience that has remained the stuff of legend.

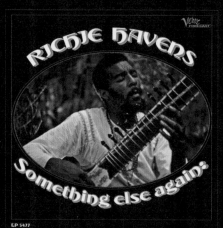

Given the decidedly folk style of most of the artists performing on the first day, it was perhaps more appropriate that Richie Havens was the opening act instead of Sweetwater. Chip Monck, who was in charge of lighting for the festival, improvised the role of master of ceremonies and introduced the artist to the audience. He welcomed Havens on stage with the words: "Ladies and gentlemen, one of the most beautiful men in the whole world, Richie Havens." At the time, the singer had performed in venues in Greenwich Village, however, despite being managed by Albert Grossman (who was also the manager of Bob Dylan and Peter, Paul & Mary), he had achieved only critical success. This performance would catapult him into the public eye.

The self-effacing way in which Havens spoke betrayed the shock he felt on facing the sea of people spread out before his eyes. Nevertheless, he did not lose his nerve, and he kept the enormous crowd enthralled with his sublime voice and primal guitar playing, backed only by his percussionist and a discreet but effective second guitarist.

Because the other groups were still struggling to reach the festival site, the organizers asked Havens to extend his set to gain some time. So he played all the songs he knew. He even launched into impromptu versions of Beatles songs—and although he knew neither all the words nor all the chords, he improvised them from memory. Legend has run wild in regards to the length of his performance, with some going so far as to describe a three-hour marathon. Although there is no way of knowing the truth, it was likely less than that—even though on stage, looking out at the audience, it must have felt like a particularly long time. At the end, Havens improvised one final song from scratch, one that was to become legendary and plunged him into a deep trance: the superb "Freedom." Thus, the festival began with one of the finest examples of spontaneous musical composition.

SETLIST

"From the Prison" / "Let's Get Together" (Hayley Mills) / "From the Prison"
(reprise) / "Minstrel From Gault" / "I'm a Stranger Here" / "High Flying Bird"
(Judy Hensk) / "I Can't Make It Anymore" / "With a Little Help from My
Friends" (The Beatles) / "Handsome Johnny" / "Strawberry Fields Forever" /
"Hey Jude" (The Beatles) / "Freedom"

THE GROUP

Richie Havens (vocals, guitar) / **Paul "Deano" Williams** (guitar) /
Daniel Ben Zebulon (percussion) / **High point:** "Freedom" / **Discography in
August 1969:** *Mixed Bag* (1966) / *Something Else Again* (1968) / *Electric Havens*
(1968) / *Richie Havens' Record* (1968) / *Richard P. Havens, 1983* (1969)

Friday
5:07 p.m.
45 minutes

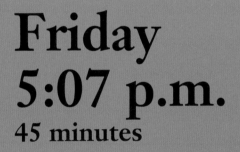

RICHIE
HAVENS

MOMENT OF GRACE

Richie Havens plays the festival's first gig. The position of his left hand, with the thumb above the guitar's fingerboard, is a highly personal technique. He is accompanied by the second guitarist, Paul "Deano" Williams, left. He, too, plays a Guild guitar, smaller than Havens's and with a microphone above the sound hole.

Swami Satchidananda, a spiritual master from India, was supposed to open the festival with his blessing, but he arrived late because of the difficulty accessing the site due to traffic. His address, which took on increasing importance as the festival progressed, was thus delivered after Richie Havens's opening performance.

The presence of Swami Satchidananda at the Woodstock festival, like the great "Hare Krishna" banner that adorned the front of the stage, were powerful symbols of the strong interest the hippie generation had in Eastern wisdom. (The words "Hare Krishna" are the best-known Hindu mantra, addressed to the supreme god, Krishna.) The poets of the Beat Generation paved the way in the 1950s—Allen Ginsberg's poem "Sunflower Sutra" dates from 1955—presenting India and Hinduism as alternatives to the materialism and triumphant capitalism of the postwar years. In music, The Beatles—and George Harrison in particular—spread the word, and in 1965 the artists included a sitar in the song "Norwegian Wood". In 1967, they met the guru Maharishi Mahesh Yogi and learned Transcendental Meditation with him. Many followed in their footsteps, including Stevie Wonder, Mick Jagger, Donovan, Moby, and David Lynch.

Swami Satchidananda, sitting on a pedestal in the lotus position, was surrounded by some 20 young hippies in saris who had attended to pray with him. The audience was now assembled into a gigantic crowd, already galvanized by its own size and a growing awareness of being part of a historic event. Satchidananda began with, "I am overwhelmed with joy to see the entire youth of America gathered here in the name of the fine art of music." These words may have seemed like hyperbole, but half a million young people gathered together did give the impression that an entire generation had been assembled, all the more so because many had traveled from the West Coast.

The rest of the spiritual master's address explained the country's crucial role in the spiritual enlightenment of the whole world (as if the United States did not already feel it was on a mission to save the rest of the world) and highlighted the contradiction in the expression "Fight for Peace"—for if you fight, you cannot find peace. To conclude, the whole audience joined Swami Satchidananda in the prayer Hari Om, and the festival truly go

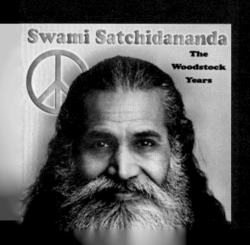

SRI SWAMI SATCHI DANANDA

Friday
6:00 p.m.
20 minutes

Sweetwater should have been the first group to mount the Woodstock stage, but traffic congestion stretching for tens of miles around forced the group to delay its set until after that of Richie Havens and Swami Satchidananda's blessing. It was still one of the first—and least predictable—groups to appear on stage at Bethel.

A rriving on stage, the bass player, by way of an excuse, quipped, "We were supposed to be on first today, but they gave us a police escort here, and the man had to stop and bust us all before he could escort us here." The joke was a way of showing the hippies in the audience that the members of Sweetwater were kindred spirits. Sweetwater was the archetypal psychedelic group of the second half of the 1960s. A West Coast group from Los Angeles, they had tried to explore new musical avenues while remaining within a fairly traditional folk rock idiom. Their eponymous first album is particularly memorable for its excellent vocal harmonies.

What's more, Sweetwater did not have a guitarist. It seemed they were the only western group at the time not to include the powerful instrument in their lineup, the ultimate symbol of the priority they gave to the collective over the individual. Each member was there to contribute to the overall sound without standing out with a solo.

The group struck up "Motherless Child," which is also the song that opens its album. Richie Havens' improvisation of "Freedom," with which he had just ended his set, had included the words of this traditional song, which produced an interesting linking effect. The members of Sweetwater had not seen the earlier set and therefore could not have known this, but it clearly shows the shared influences at the festival.

"Motherless Child" (traditional) / "Look Out" / "For Pete's Sake" / "Day Song" /
"What's Wrong" / "My Crystal Spider" / "Two Worlds" / "Why, Oh Why?" /
"Let the Sunshine In" (The 5th Dimension) / "Oh Happy Day" (traditional)

SWEET WATER

Friday
6:30 p.m.
45 minutes

THE GROUP

Nancy Nevins (vocals) / Fred Herrera (bass guitar) / Alex Del Zoppo
(keyboards) / Alan Malarowitz (drums) / August Burns (cello) / Elpidio
"Pete" Cobian (percussion) / Albert Moore (flute, percussion) / High point:
"Motherless Child" / Discography in August 1969: *Sweetwater* (1968)

PERCUSSIVE

Elpidio "Pete" Cobian was the drummer of the group Sweetwater. He is seen here holding his tambourine. During the rest of the gig, he also played the congas, which are visible in the foreground. This mic, a Shure Unisphere I Model 565, which cost one hundred dollars at the time, was used by all the artists at the festival.

Bert Sommer was not well known to the general public, so he was not playing to an audience of fans, although his folk style was perfectly in keeping with the general tone of this first day. Nonetheless, after the disorganized psychedelia of Sweetwater, the simplicity of his folk music brought a big breath of fresh air.

S weetwater's penultimate number was "Let the Sunshine In," the final song of the hippie musical *Hair* (released in 1967). By an extraordinary coincidence, the next artist to go onto the Woodstock stage had gotten his big break by playing Woof in the Broadway production of *Hair* in 1968. Indeed, his superb Afro hairstyle had featured on the musical's program at the time.

Bert Sommer, then barely 20 years old—as evidenced by his youthful baby face—played a Gibson J-200 at Woodstock in a style reminiscent of David Crosby. The group that played with him was reduced to the bare minimum, lacking even a drummer. The bass player, Charlie Bilello, provided a well-grounded, solid foundation, while Ira Stone embellished the songs with discreet, jazzy notes. He was one of those great accompanists who had the gift of making a song better without taking all the credit. However, history has largely forgotten him—as it has Bert Sommer. Sommer was not included either in the movie or the record made of the festival and, consequently, did not benefit from the exposure that these would have provided.

Most of the songs in his performance were his own compositions, largely drawn from his first album and, although the original studio versions are more thoroughly arranged, they did not suffer in that more simple setting. The magnificent cover of "America" reminded the audience that Simon & Garfunkel were not on the festival's bill, although they would have fitted in perfectly. However, relations had deteriorated between Paul and Art, who would go their separate ways the following year. Night fell, and Bert left the stage to make way for another genius folk singer.

BERT SOMMER
THE ROAD TO TRAVEL

BERT SOMMER

Friday
7:30 p.m.
40 minutes

"Jennifer" / "The Road to Travel" / "I Wondered Where You'd Be" / "She's Gone" / "Things Are Going My Way" / "And When It's Over" / "Jeanette" / "America" (Simon & Garfunkel) / "A Note That Read" / "Smile"

THE GROUP

Bert Sommer (vocals, guitar) / **Ira Stone** (lead guitar, organ) / **Charlie Bilello** (bass guitar) / **High point:** "Jennifer" / **Discography in August 1969:** *The Road to Travel* (1968)

SETLIST

"(How Can We) Hang On to a Dream" / "Susan" / "If I Were a Carpenter" / "Reason to Believe" / "You Upset the Grace of Living When You Lie" / "Speak Like a Child" / "Snow White Lady" / "Blues On the Ceiling" (Fred Neil) / "Simple Song of Freedom" (Bobby Darin) / "Misty Roses"

THE GROUP

Tim Hardin (vocals, guitar, piano) / **Gilles Malkine** (guitar) / **Ralph Towner** (guitar, piano) / **Glen Moore** (double bass) / **Bill Chelf** (piano) / **Steve "Muruga" Booker** (drums) / **Richard Bock** (cello) / **High point:** *"If I Were a Carpenter"* / **Discography in August 1969:** *Tim Hardin 1* (1966) / *Tim Hardin 2* (1967) / *This Is Tim Hardin* (1967) / *Tim Hardin 3 Live in Concert* (1968) / *Tim Hardin 4* (1969) / *Suite for Susan Moore and Damion: We Are One, One, All in One* (1969)

Friday
9:00 p.m.
35 minutes

TIM HARDIN

Accounts differ as to when Tim Hardin should have played at Woodstock festival. Some sources claim he was meant to be the first artist to go on stage, in place of Richie Havens; others say he simply made way for Bert Sommer and eventually decided to play late at nightfall. The only certainty is that he played later than planned.

I t was widely known that Hardin was a heroin addict since his experience as a marine in Vietnam in the early 1960s. The drug finally cost him his life in 1980. At Woodstock, it may be that an injection taken too recently had rendered him incapable of singing at the originally appointed time; he may simply have been experiencing stage fright, faced with the size of the audience that awaited him. Anyway, the two suggested explanations for his delay are not incompatible, and it is entirely conceivable that heroin did not help the singer's paranoia. Nonetheless, his performance was a highlight of that folk-themed first day.

NEAR MISSES

Tim Hardin was a brilliant star of the Greenwich Village folk scene. Throughout his career, however, he had brushes with success without ever truly achieving it: Columbia had canceled his contract in 1964, but then signed him again in 1969; his only hit single was one of his few covers ("Simple Song of Freedom" by Bobby Darin); and he gave far fewer concerts than his peers for the reasons given above. Nevertheless, Bob Dylan said of him that he was the greatest living singer-songwriter. The songs he wrote often became hits on albums by other artists, such as Bobby Darin (again), Joan Baez with "If I Were a Carpenter," and Rod Stewart with "Reason to Believe." Hardin's demons often prevented him from seizing opportunities, including being the first musician to play at Woodstock, which was apparently suggested by his friend Michael Lang as a way of exposing him to a wide, attentive audience.

MISTY ROSES

Hardin finally went on stage at 9:00 p.m. and performed one of his finest songs: "(How Can We) Hang On to a Dream." He sang with a voice full of authority and charisma—the first truly great voice at Woodstock— and was accompanied by only his pianist Bill Chelf. The rest of the group,

BLACK SHEEP BOY
AN INTRODUCTION TO
TIM HARDIN

Suite For Susan Moore and Damion –
We Are – One. One, All In One
Bird On A Wire

which was made up essentially of jazz virtuosi (the guitarist Ralph Towner, the double bass player Glen Moore, and the drummer Steve Booker were among the big names on the scene at the time), knew how to keep a low profile when their presence was not required. Being accompanied by jazz musicians instead of folk or rock musicians proved to be a shrewd strategic decision by Hardin, because the subtlety of his group allowed for him to display all the nuances of his voice without being drowned out by excessively loud musicians.

For the sublime "If I Were a Carpenter," he was alone with his acoustic guitar, and nothing was lacking. Hardin thus perfectly demonstrated the beauty of the sparseness and restraint of a well-written song. His most recent album at the time, the highly experimental *Suite For Susan Moore and Damion: We Are One, One, All In One*, was released two months earlier. It featured a mixture of the spoken word and jazz—and it was veritable commercial suicide. Only one of its songs, "Susan," was played at Woodstock to make way for numbers with a more traditional format, drawn from his first two albums. There was also an excellent cover of "Blues on the Ceiling" by the New York bluesman Fred Neil, proof that Hardin was capable of moving from one style to another with equal grace.

His set finally concluded with the superb "Misty Roses." As he ended the song, the weekend's first storm broke, transforming the festival site into a world of mud, which the hippies took to with gusto.

Ravi Shankar never made a secret of his bemusement of the hippie movement, yet it made him into a superstar. The sitar virtuoso did much to popularize Indian classical music in the West—through his many concerts in the United States and Europe, his albums, and, above all, through his friendship with George Harrison.

T he albums made by Shankar himself met with only modest success (although, with 18 albums released in less than ten years, Shankar was in the record stores all the same). His greatest exposure came thanks to The Beatles' use of the sitar, and also through Shankar's participation in the two festivals that defined the time: the 1967 Monterey Pop Festival and Woodstock in 1969. At Monterey, he almost canceled his performance, having got wind of the ritual destruction of instruments wreaked by The Who and Jimi Hendrix, who were also on the bill. For a musician who came from a tradition as religious as that of Indian ragas, the sitar was not a mere material tool but a way of gaining access to divinity—and therefore, by extension, an inseparable part of that divinity.

There was this same mutual incomprehension at Woodstock. In his autobiography, Shankar would even compare the festivalgoers in the mud to the water buffalo of his native India. He was shocked by the way hippies automatically linked music with drugs, and he got the impression that his music, instead of captivating the audience, had merely served as the backdrop to a joyful party. From the festivalgoers' point of view, Shankar was seen as a pretext, a prerequisite for proving one's musical open-mindedness, but most of them only really explored Indian music through The Byrds' borrowings. After three numbers, including an eight-minute tabla (Indian percussion) solo, Ravi Shankar left the stage to make way for an artist more in tune with the audience.

RAVI SHANKAR

SETLIST

"Raga Puriya-Dhanashri/Gat in Sawarital" / "Tabla Solo in Jhaptal" /
"Raga Manj Khamaj"

THE GROUP

Ravi Shankar (sitar) / **Maya Kulkarni** (tambura) / **Ustad Alla Rakha** (tabla) /
High point: "Raga Puriya-Dhanashri/Gat in Sawarital" / **Discography in
August 1969:** *Three Ragas* (1956) / *Music of India* (1962) / *Improvisations*
(1962) / *India's Most Distinguished Musician in Concert* (1962) / *Ravi Shankar*
(1963) / *India's Master Musician* (1963) / *In London* (1964) / *Ragas & Talas* (1964) /
Portrait of Genius (1964) / *Sound of the Sitar* (1965) / *In San Francisco* (1967) /
The Exotic Sitar and Sarod (1967) / *Two Raga Moods* (1967) / *Live: Ravi Shankar
at the Monterey International Pop Festival* (1967) / *A Morning Raga/An Evening
Raga* (1968) / *The Sounds of India* (1968) / *A Sitar Recital* (1968) / *Ravi Shankar
Improvisations & Theme from Pather Panchali* (1968) / *Ravi Shankar's Festival
From India* (1968) / *Ravi Shankar* (1969)

Melanie was one of the festival's wonderful anomalies. She performed between Ravi Shankar and Arlo Guthrie, two prominent symbols of the hippie movement—whereas she was almost unknown at the time. She had only one album to her name, *Born To Be*, which had not sold well.

Melanie arrived on New York's Greenwich Village scene at a time when the wider public had already shifted its attention to the West Coast. She found herself at Woodstock thanks to a set of circumstances that was as lucky as it was unlikely. First of all, her office was in the same building as that of the festival organizers, who suggested she take part. Second, The Incredible String Band, who were scheduled to play in that time slot, refused to play in the rain (they would finally play the following day).

At the age of 22, Melanie, alone with her classical guitar (she was one of the few folk singers to choose nylon strings over steel), faced the crowd of 500,000 people who were soaked to the skin. She played for only around 25 minutes, but her charm worked immediately. She instantly created a special mood that was both familiar in its format (short, solo folk songs) and radically original in its interpretation. The quality of her voice was unlike any other, not only in its timbre, which contained traditional Irish influences, but in her choice of notes, her vibrato, and her way of lengthening certain syllables, even in a song as well known as Bob Dylan's "Mr. Tambourine Man" (incidentally, this was the first reminder of the great absentee).

The audience, to whom Melanie called out in "Animal Crackers," understood that something rare was going on, and it lit cigarette lighters, matches, and candles to convey its support to the singer, despite the rain. The memory of this moment of communion was later to bring forth "Lay Down (Candles in the Rain)," the 1970 single that would be the singer's greatest hit. Despite being left out of the movie, Melanie was still one of the artists for whom Woodstock was a decisive turning point.

Friday
11:00 p.m.
25 minutes

MELANIE

SETLIST

"Close to It All" / "Momma Momma" / "Beautiful People" / "Animal Crackers" /
"Mr. Tambourine Man" (Bob Dylan) / "Tuning My Guitar" / "Birthday of the Sun"

THE GROUP

Melanie Safka (vocals, guitar) / **High point:** "Birthday of the Sun" /
Discography in August 1969: *Born To Be* (1968),
renamed *My First Album* when she became successful

Although he had released only a small number of records at the time he played at Woodstock, Arlo Guthrie was among the best-known artists playing on that first day. As the son of the singer Woody Guthrie, who had been the chief influence on Bob Dylan, his surname was already famous, and he had ensured that his first name was known in 1967 with his first album.

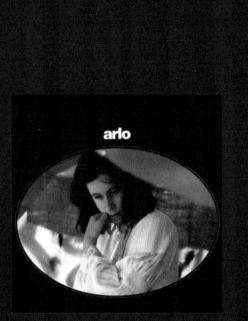

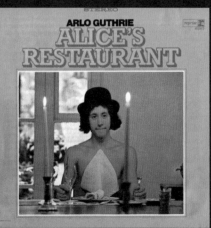

The first track on this album, the 18-minute-long "Alice's Restaurant Massacree," takes up the whole of the first side and had become a widely celebrated song. This talking blues song (in the Greenwich Village tradition, from which Arlo Guthrie came) tells the comical story of a man arrested by the police for dumping garbage in the wrong place. This openly anti-Vietnam War and antiestablishment song is still a Thanksgiving tradition for many Americans.

However, Arlo Guthrie did not sing "Alice's Restaurant Massacree" at Woodstock. For one thing, the huge setting of the concert did not necessarily lend itself to a song lasting almost 20 minutes, and also, his psychedelically drugged state would not have helped him to remember the lyrics of such a tour de force. In its place, Arlo Guthrie launched into two songs, "Coming into Los Angeles" and "Wheel of Fortune," and then followed these with covers—two traditional, and most notably his version of Bob Dylan's "Walkin' Down the Line." Not only did he choose a completely obscure song that only the most knowledgeable Dylan fans would have recognized (it was recorded for a magazine and Dylan's publisher, but it was never released on an album), but he introduced it by saying, "We're gonna do a Bobby Dylan tune. Maybe he'll do it with us, maybe he won't." Arlo Guthrie seemed as surprised as the audience at the absence of the hermit of the nearby West Saugerties.

Finally, Arlo Guthrie's performance is famous for his announcement that the freeway from New York had been closed because of the massive influx of festivalgoers. This was false, but the romantic fantasy prevailed over the truth.

"Coming into Los Angeles" / "Wheel of Fortune" / "Walkin' Down the Line"
(Bob Dylan) / "Arlo Speech: Exodus" / "Oh Mary Don't You Weep" (traditional) /
"Every Hand in the Land" / "Amazing Grace" (traditional)

Friday
11:55 p.m.
30 minutes

ARLO GUTHRIE

Arlo Guthrie (vocals, guitar) / John Pilla (guitar) / Bob Arkin (bass guitar) /
Paul Motian (drums) / High point: "Coming into Los Angeles" /
Discography in August 1969: *Alice's Restaurant* (1967) / *Arlo* (1968) /
Running Down the Road (1969)

Saturday
1:00 a.m.
60 minutes

JOAN BAEZ

SETLIST

"**Oh Happy Day**" (traditional) / "**The Last Thing on My Mind**" (Tom Paxton) /
"**I Shall Be Released**" (Bob Dylan) / "**No Expectations**" (The Rolling Stones) /
"**Joe Hill**" (Earl Robinson) / "**Sweet Sir Galahad**" / "**Hickory Wind**" (The Byrds) /
"**Drug Store Truck Drivin' Man**" (The Byrds) / "**One Day at a Time**" (Willie
Nelson) / "**Take Me Back to the Sweet Sunny South**" / "**Warm and Tender
Love**" (Joe Haywood) / "**Swing Low, Sweet Chariot**" (traditional) /
"**We Shall Overcome**" (traditional)

THE GROUP

Joan Baez (vocals, guitar) / **Richard Festinger** (guitar) / **Jeffrey Shurtleff** (guitar,
vocals) / **High point:** "Swing Low, Sweet Chariot" / **Discography in August 1969:**
Joan Baez (1960) / *Joan Baez, Vol. 2* (1961) / *Joan Baez in Concert* (1962) /
Joan Baez In Concert, Part 2 (1963) / *Joan Baez/5* (1964) / *Farewell, Angelina*
(1965) / *Noël* (1965) / *Joan* (1967) / *Baptism: A Journey Through Our Time*
(1968) / *Any Day Now* (1968) / *David's Album* (1969)

Joan Baez concluded the Friday's performances with a memorable set, worthy of her reputation as a folk superstar. Perfectly balancing the sweetness of her voice with the power of her convictions, Baez was the ultimate protest singer and totally in her element at Woodstock.

I t would be reductive and false to see Joan Baez solely as Bob Dylan's ex and his muse of the 1960s, at a time when they were the first couple of Greenwich Village and an alliance of two leaders in that microcosm. Contrary to what people might imagine—given how Dylan's career took off afterward—Baez's career began well beforehand, with her first album in 1960. It was she who was on the cover of *Time Magazine* in 1962, she who invited Dylan to sing a few songs at her concerts when he was a complete unknown, and she who invited him to join her in March 1963, when she went to sing at the March on Washington after Martin Luther King Jr.'s famous speech. However, although she performed many of Dylan's songs, and imitated his spoken voice to perfection, there was much more to Joan Baez than that.

This singer, with her crystal-clear voice and guitar playing as delicate as lace, was one of the pioneers of the Greenwich Village folk scene, and she has remained the most honest and faithful to this ideal all her life. Now, almost 60 years after the start of her career, she still tours the world over, alone with her guitar, her voice almost unchanged. Her convictions have not changed either, and Baez has not stopped fighting for important social causes, right up to her participation in 2011's Occupy Wall Street movement.

PREGNANT AND ANGRY

When she mounted the stage at the Woodstock festival to bring its first day to a close, Joan Baez was six months pregnant, and her husband, the activist David Harris, had been in jail for two months. She had met him in jail, while he was serving a previous sentence and Baez was imprisoned for blocking the entrance to a military recruitment center. The two were married on their release. David Harris was then jailed again in June 1969 for refusing to join the army. Between a rendition of "I Shall Be Released" that was filled with hope (Harris would indeed be released from jail in

It wasn't any fucking revolution; it was a three-day period during which people were decent to one another because they realized that if they weren't, they'd all get hungry.

Joan Baez

September 1970) and a sadly prophetic "No Expectations" (the couple would divorce in 1973), Baez told with anger and determination the story of her husband's arrest. The two musicians who came on stage to accompany her in the cover of The Byrds' "Drug Store Truck Drivin' Man" were fellow activists with David Harris. Jeffrey Shurtleff sang, played acoustic guitar, and dedicated the song to Ronald Reagan, whom he accused of being close to the Ku Klux Klan, while Richard Festinger punctuated the whole song with subtle, well-judged phrases on the electric guitar.

Along with all this, Baez explored the Greenwich Village repertoire (Tom Paxton's "The Last Thing on My Mind" and Dylan's "I Shall Be Released"), but also alternative country music (The Byrds, Willie Nelson), rhythm 'n' blues, and film music (Earl Robinson). From this medley of styles, rendered perfectly coherent thanks to Baez's voice, what stood out most were the three songs borrowed from the gospel repertoire: the opening number "Oh Happy Day," a deeply moving "Swing Low, Sweet Chariot," which she sang solo and unaccompanied, and the finale "We Shall Overcome." For that last song, a veritable anthem of the civil rights struggle, Joan Baez spoke each phrase before singing it to encourage the audience to join her in chorus. Despite the lateness of the hour and a relentless drizzle, she created a powerful moment of communion to bring that first day to a close.

S
A

SATURDAY, AUGUST 16, 1969

FROM SATURDAY 12:15 P.M.
TO SUNDAY 8:00 A.M.

The first group to appear on stage on the second day was totally unknown, although it deserved to have been more successful. Quill was a New England group that had built a solid reputation locally by being the warm-up act for the many groups that passed through the region.

Despite torrential rain and the arrival of the Hells Angels at about 4:00 a.m., the first night at Woodstock passed without any problems, and the 500,000 people who had formed a new kind of town were learning to cohabit. Even the potential violence of the Hells Angels had been neutralized by the gentleness of the general ambiance and the unreal quality of the assembled crowd. The morning announcements dealt with obtaining food, hygiene, and the quality of the drugs in circulation. "Now, people been saying that some of the acid is poison. It's not poison, it's just bad acid." Hence the organizers' wise and reasonable advice: "If you feel like experimenting, only take half a tab, okay?"

Quill's refined and intelligent progressive rock brought to mind Spirit and Iron Butterfly, as well as early Blood, Sweat & Tears, which showed more pronounced blues influences. From the first notes they played, it was clear that the group was accustomed to being on stage, and on small stages where conditions were not always ideal. Despite a sound system that was far from being up to the task, the musicians immediately got into the spirit of things, and the vocal harmonies of their 10-minute composition "They Live the Life" were faultless. This technical perfection was just the start, and Quill played with an impressive groove and skilled riffs. Because of a technical issue, however, their performance could not be included in the movie, and Quill thus remained Woodstock's unknown group. They certainly deserved better. The group's eponymous album, released in 1970, was perfectly competent, but it lacked the energy and enthusiasm that can be heard on the recordings of the Woodstock concert. Justice was finally done to the group in 2009 with the release of the compilation *Woodstock 40 Years On: Back to Yasgur's Farm*, which includes the first two songs of the group's set.

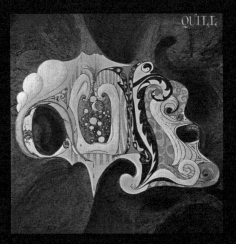

Dan Cole (vocals, trombone) / **Norman Rogers** (guitar) / **Jon Cole** (bass guitar, vocals) / **Phil Thayer** (keyboards, saxophone, flute) / **Roger North** (drums) / **High point:** "They Live the Life" / **Discography in August 1969:** No albums

QUILL

Saturday 12:15 p.m.
40 minutes

SETLIST

"They Live the Life" / **"That's How I Eat"** / **"Driftin' Blues"** (Johnny Moore's Three Blazers) / **"Waitin' for You"**

COUNTRY JOE MCDONALD

Saturday
1:00 p.m.
30 minutes

Country Joe McDonald (vocals, guitar) / **High point:** The "FISH" cheer /
Discography in August 1969 (with The Fish): *Electric Music for the Mind and Body* (1967) / *I-Feel-Like-I'm-Fixin'-to-Die* (1967) / *Together* (1968) / *Here We Are Again* (1969)

SETLIST

"Janis" / "Donovan's Reef" / "Heartaches by the Number" (Guy Mitchell) /
"Ring of Fire" (Johnny Cash) / "Tennessee Stud" (Jimmy Driftwood) /
"Rockin' Round the World" / "Flying High" / "I Seen a Rocket" /
The "FISH" cheer / "I-Feel-Like-I'm-Fixin'-to-Die Rag"

Country Joe McDonald's acoustic solo performance is one of those moments that immediately brings to mind the Woodstock festival. The image of the singer, with his long hair and moustache, wearing a military jacket and bandana, has entered the collective unconscious of the hippie movement.

The appearance of Country Joe McDonald was one of the last-minute surprises sprung by the organizers. At first, Michael Lang was unwilling to include Country Joe & The Fish, the psychedelic group from Berkeley, California, in the program on the pretext that he did not want to include openly political groups. However, given the unambiguous political commitment of other artists at the festival (such as Joan Baez, Arlo Guthrie, and Sly Stone), it can be assumed that Lang simply wasn't a fan of the group's music; its value, it has to be said, lays more in its message than in its originality. They may have been part of the same movement, but Country Joe & The Fish were not in the same league as Jefferson Airplane, Grateful Dead, or The Doors.

SURPRISE

Because Jeff Beck canceled his performance, the organizers had to fill the gap left by this headliner. Thanks to the funds released by Beck's departure, they were able to add two groups to the program: The Paul Butterfield Blues Band and Country Joe & The Fish. Although the latter group was scheduled for Sunday afternoon, Santana's equipment was not yet in place on Saturday and a gap needed to be filled. The organizers hurried to the dressing rooms, where they came upon Country Joe McDonald and managed to persuade him to play a solo set. However, there was one problem: he did not have a guitar with him. Bill Belmont, Country Joe's manager, tells the story: "I told John [Morris, the festival's production coordinator], 'We need a guitar.' Someone walked on stage with a guitar, so we took it and found a piece of rope to act as a strap. We gave him the guitar and he said, 'You call that a guitar?' [the instrument in question was a cheap Yamaha]. Then I pushed him on stage."

In 1968, the members of Country Joe & The Fish were, from left: Mark Kapner (keyboards), Country Joe McDonald (guitar, vocals), Barry "The Fish" Melton (standing; guitar, vocals), Greg Dewey (drums), and Doug Metzler (bass guitar).

In a fine illustration of the camaraderie among musicians at the festival, three members of Jefferson Airplane (the bass player Jack Casady, wearing glasses and a bandana; the singer Grace Slick, also wearing glasses; and the mustached drummer Spencer Dryden, along with a female friend) sit together while Country Joe McDonald stands beside them with the promoter Bill Graham.

WHOOPEE

On top of his hasty arrival on stage, it turned out that Country Joe was not used to giving solo concerts—something that is a daunting prospect, especially in front of 500,000 people. Under the circumstances, a forgettable performance could be easily excused. He alternated between songs written by his own group and country music classics—not a style that was typically popular among hippies on account of its association with conservative politics. The audience showed no interest in the performance until Bill Belmont suggested to Joe that he conclude his set with Country Joe & The Fish's best-known song, "I-Feel-Like-I'm-Fixin'-to-Die Rag."

As was his custom, Joe introduced this piece with the "FISH" cheer. Borrowed from cheerleaders at sports games, this was a technique for warming up an audience in which the members are asked to spell the group's name. Usually, Joe would get an audience to spell out "FISH," but this time he asked it: "Gimme an F! Gimme a U! Gimme a C! Gimme a K! What do you get?" And the audience replied, in a collective roar: "FUCK!" Thus the "FISH" cheer became the "FUCK" cheer—a truly historic moment. Country Joe then went straight into the song properly, a folk novelty song in which the audience's participation was made easier by the use of numbers in the chorus: "And it's one, two, three, what are we fightin' for?/Don't ask me, I don't give a damn/The next stop is Vietnam/And it's five, six, seven, open up the Pearly Gates!/Well, there ain't no time to wonder why/Whoopee! We're all gonna die!" The protest song form has rarely been as effective as on that Saturday afternoon.

SETLIST

"Waiting" / "Evil Ways" (Willie Bobo) / "You Just Don't Care" / "Savor" /
"Jingo" (Babatunde Olatunji) / "Persuasion" / "Soul Sacrifice" /
"Fried Neckbones and Some Home Fries" (Willie Bobo)

SANTANA

Saturday 2:00 p.m.
45 minutes

THE GROUP

Carlos Santana (lead guitar) / **Gregg Rolie** (vocals, organ, percussion) /
David Brown (bass guitar) / **Michael Shrieve** (drums) / **Jose "Chepito"
Areas** (percussion, trumpet) / **Michael Carabello** (congas) / **High point:**
"Soul Sacrifice" / **Discography in August 1969:** No albums

Of all the revelations of Woodstock festival, Santana was without a doubt the most unexpected—and lasting. The group's presence was the subject of heated arguments over programming, with some not understanding how part of the budget could be allocated to an unknown group that had not yet released an album.

B ill Graham, a key figure in the music world at the time, nevertheless had the last word. Among his numerous areas of activity (he founded Fillmore Records, a label that signed up Rod Stewart and Elvin Bishop, and he managed Jefferson Airplane from their beginnings until 1968), it was his talent as a concert promoter that had, by far, the greatest impact. He made the Fillmore Auditorium famous, then he established two legendary auditoriums: the Fillmore East (in New York) and the Fillmore West (in San Francisco). Thanks to him, groups such as The Paul Butterfield Blues Band, Big Brother & The Holding Company, and Country Joe & The Fish were able to find an audience while retaining a committed radical stance as artists. And, of course, Graham also played a big part in the success of the Grateful Dead, a group he always supported and which he was promoting at the time of Woodstock. The organizers wanted the Dead, but Graham was prepared to grant their wish only on the condition that they also agreed to welcome his small group of protégés—a tried-and-tested approach. So it was thanks to Bill Graham's blackmail that Santana found themselves on the bill at Woodstock. Graham even found his way on stage during Santana's concert, and he can be seen playing a cowbell, leaning back against Gregg Rolie's Leslie speaker.

AMBITIOUS YOUNGSTERS

At the time, Santana was a group much more than an individual. Over time, however, Carlos Santana, the group's guitarist and founder, took on such importance that he became its sole public face. But, in 1969, he was at the head of a veritable collective of musical adventurers. The group's lineup changed regularly, but at the time of Woodstock it settled around Carlos and Gregg Rolie (singer, organist, and co-founder of the group). Michael Shrieve was on drums, and he could boast that he was both the youngest musician to have played at Woodstock—he was just 20 years old at the time of the performance—and the drummer who would be

Carlos Santana at the height of his trip on the Woodstock stage. The machine heads on his Gibson SG have been replaced by Grover tuners.

Carlos Santana rings a bell to complement his group's percussion arsenal. The bass player David Brown is on the left, while the two percussionists, Jose "Chepito" Areas and Mike Carabello (with the Afro hairstyle), are on the right, behind the congas, adding a real rhythmic drive to Santana's music.

best remembered by the festivalgoers, thanks to his staggering solo on "Soul Sacrifice." Michael Carabello and Jose Areas were the group's two percussionists, and they brought a Latin flavor that was unheard of in rock music at the time. Finally, David Brown took care of underpinning and reconciling all these fine people with his bass lines of rare intelligence.

Carlos Santana himself was a fascinating phenomenon, a unique guitarist whom no one has tried to imitate since. He seemed to master the electricity of each note directly, without any intermediary, and to seek his melodies in distant spheres, starting with blues and ending up with John Coltrane-like free jazz (Babatunde Olatunji, who composed "Jin-Go-Lo-Ba," retitled "Jingo" for Santana's cover, was a close friend of the wonderful saxophonist). On stage at Woodstock, Carlos played with the energy and inventiveness of an up-and-coming genius who still had everything to prove. He had just turned 22 years old, played in front of 500,000 people, and explored a musical direction that Jimi Hendrix would struggle to find the following day.

Communication within the group was excellent, which incidentally helps explains the quality of its performance. The artists could be seen exchanging knowing looks—signs for developing their collective improvisations—and smiles of satisfaction at the superb sound they were creating together. There is no doubt that the situation would have seemed to them as surreal as it was undreamed of, because, just five days earlier, they had played for a student organization in New York.

INSPIRED

When the group went on stage, Carlos Santana found himself the victim of an organizational blunder. The group had arrived at the festival site at around 11:00 a.m. that morning and was told it would play at about 8:00 p.m. So Carlos decided he had time to take the mescaline he had brought with him, and that he would have enough time to come down by the time the group was due to play. But, because of the festival's slightly anarchic organization, Carlos found himself playing with the group at 2:00 p.m., at the peak of his trip. Mescaline is a Mexican drug extracted from cacti, and its effects are similar to those of LSD. It enables the user to see geometric and kaleidoscopic shapes, and to develop synesthesia (the capacity to associate music with colors, among other things). We can only imagine what kind of experience that concert would have been for Carlos. When people saw the way his face twisted and convulsed at the sound of certain notes, they doubted whether, in his head, they were just notes, or

open doors into the cosmos. Several decades afterward, Carlos said that the neck of his guitar felt like "an electric snake" that wouldn't stay still, and his facial contortions were because he was trying to control the snake and make it stand still.

From the opening of the instrumental number "Waiting," the electric snake produced sounds that were sometimes soft, sometimes piercing—but always brilliant. Two songs by the Latin jazz genius Willie Bobo were included in the set along with the group's own compositions. Santana had just recorded their first album and, among these compositions, "Soul Sacrifice" is remembered as a highlight of the festival. This instrumental number has become one of those moments that people knew would go down in history—the birth of a phenomenon in public. Fifty years and more than 100 million albums sold later, Santana remains one of the most enduring legends of 1969.

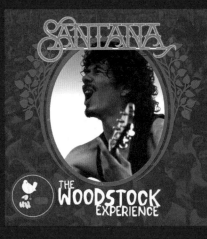

Just as Country Joe McDonald found himself being called up at the last minute to keep the audience occupied while Santana's equipment was being set up, someone was also needed to fill the gap while it was being taken down. This time it was John Sebastian who agreed to fill in— although he had originally arrived at the festival as a member of the audience.

T he contrast between this musician and Santana was striking. Sebastian had already achieved considerable success with his group, The Lovin' Spoonful, which had released six albums over three years, before he left the group to devote himself to his solo career. At the young age of 25, Sebastian was already a veteran.

Nevertheless, his was not a half-hearted performance and, although Sebastian played only five songs in an extremely laid-back manner (accounts differ on whether cannabis or acid was responsible), he gave his all, establishing a communication with the audience. After "Darlin' Be Home Soon," his generosity was rewarded by an unambiguous request for more. The audience was not asking just to be polite. It was a truly overwhelming demand for this artist, who was not used to playing solo (he had given only three solo concerts before, in Washington in January 1969). His first three songs were compositions he would record for his first solo album, *John B. Sebastian* (January 1970); the last two were Lovin' Spoonful classics. The decision to end with "Younger Generation" was far from an accident. This superb song is a reflection on the generation gap and the idea that "every generation thinks their folks are square." In the last two verses, he imagines what his child will say to him: "What's the matter Daddy, how come you're turning green?/Can it be that you can't live up to your dreams?" And Sebastian concluded with these words, which were not in the original song: "It's not true, because we're doin' it!" Woodstock was the fulfillment of his generation's dream, and John Sebastian found the perfect words for it.

JOHN SEBAS TIAN

Saturday
3:30 p.m.
25 minutes

"How Have You Been" / "Rainbows All Over Your Blues" / "I Had a Dream" /
"Darlin' Be Home Soon" / "Younger Generation"

John Sebastian (vocals, guitar) / **High point:** "Younger Generation" /
Discography in August 1969 (with The Lovin' Spoonful): *Do You Believe
in Magic* (1965) / *Daydream* (1966) / *What's Up Tiger Lily?* (1966) /
Hums of the Lovin' Spoonful (1966) / *You're a Big Boy Now* (1967) /
Everything Playing (1967)

LEGENDARY

This well-known, striking photograph of the festival shows John Sebastian, seen from behind, facing the crowd of half a million people. Taken from the position of the drum kit by Henry Diltz (one of the main photographers who documented Woodstock), this shot clearly shows the huge size of the audience.

Keef Hartley was the first British person to play at the festival. Native to Lancashire, England, he was one of those musicians who had several brushes with rock's greatest legends yet never succeeded in getting his own name at the top of the bill.

KEEF HARTLEY

K

eef Hartley joined Rory Storm & The Hurricanes in 1962. Today, that group is not well known, but Hartley was replacing Ringo Starr, who had left to join The Beatles. He then became the drummer of The Artwoods, and, finally, he replaced Mick Fleetwood (who had left to found Fleetwood Mac) in John Mayall & The Bluesbreakers. The guitarists Eric Clapton, Mick Taylor, and Peter Green had each belonged to this group at various times, which was somewhat of an institution for the cream of 1960s musicians to hone their skills—the Miles Davis Quintet of British blues.

Like most of the people who had played with John Mayall, Hartley set up his own group with his former boss's blessing. Indeed, the Keef Hartley Band's first album opened with a sketch re-creating his dismissal by Mayall, and the first song was entitled "Sacked." This first album, on whose sleeve Hartley posed dressed as a Native American chief, placed him in the tradition of intellectual blues rock.

That was probably what prevented Hartley's band from making a big impression at Woodstock. The huge audience, large stage, and rather basic sound system did not give the subtlety of the band's arrangements much of a chance. The musicians began their set with the instrumental number "Spanish Fly," in which Henry Lowther's trumpet had the lion's share of the action, but their version of Latin groove was much less sensual and visceral than Santana's. The audience did not know the songs, and quickly lost interest in a group that seemed to be playing for itself; the members seemed more interested in showcasing their instrumental skills than in interacting with the front rows of the audience. This was only the tenth concert for the Keef Hartley Band since they formed in 1968, and their depth of experience was totally inadequate for the scope of their musical ambition and the huge scale of the event.

KEEF HARTLEY BAND

Saturday
4:45 p.m.
45 minutes

SETLIST

"Spanish Fly" / "Think It Over" / "She's Gone" / "Too Much Thinking" / "The Halfbreed" / "Believe In You" / "Rock Me Baby" (B.B. King) / "Sinnin' for You" (intro) / "Leaving Trunk" (Sleepy John Estes) / "Just to Cry" / "Sinnin' for You"

THE GROUP

Keef Hartley (drums) / **Miller Anderson** (vocals, guitar) / **Gary Thain** (bass guitar) / **Henry Lowther** (trumpet, violin) / **Jimmy Jewell** (saxophone) / **High point:** "Spanish Fly" / **Discography in August 1969:** *Halfbreed* (1969)

The award for the festival's ultimate Unidentified Playing Object goes without a doubt to The Incredible String Band. The audience was waiting for a blues rock onslaught from Canned Heat and Mountain, but it was a Scottish quartet that came on stage, two men and two women dressed in white.

M ike Heron and Robin Williamson shared the lead vocals, depending on the song, and traded the guitar and piano as it inspired them (in general, whoever was playing guitar sang the lead vocals). Williamson's mastery of the piano was limited, and his arrangements gave the ensemble a baroque quality, within which his rhythmic rigidity seemed sometimes deliberate, sometimes not. Rose Simpson played the bass line with a highly personal and lyrical style, which owed as much to Paul McCartney as it did to contrapuntal writing, while Christina "Licorice" McKechnie played drums—only tom-toms—using broom handles. The two of them also sang high-pitched backing vocals with an out-of-tune quality that was reminiscent of The Velvet Underground, but in a more folklike style.

The Incredible String Band's career began in 1966. The name was more apt at the start, when the group consisted of Williamson, Heron, and Clive Palmer, and it played traditional folk. After Palmer's departure, the two remaining members went in a more psychedelic, progressive, and musically complex direction, releasing albums that featured rich arrangements. The latter were far too rich for a group of four musicians to do them full justice, and The Incredible String Band also suffered from the timing of their performance. They were meant to play the previous day, which would have been more in keeping with the rest of the bill, but the group decided to postpone their performance because of rain. The Saturday was already set to be a much more intense, rock-oriented day, so the audience did not give such pieces as the superb finale, "When You Find Out Who You Are"—which combines three songs in one—a chance. When it became known, furthermore, that the group only played songs that had not yet been released on an album, it was felt that there was a fine line between a taste for musical adventure and commercial suicide.

"Invocation" (spoken word) / "The Letter" / "Gather 'Round" / "This Moment" /
"Come With Me" / "When You Find Out Who You Are"

THE INCREDIBLE STRING BAND

**Saturday
6:00 p.m.**
30 minutes

Mike Heron (vocals, guitar, piano) / **Robin Williamson** (guitar, piano, vocals, violin) /
Rose Simpson (bass guitar, flute, vocals, percussion) / **Christina "Licorice" McKechnie**
(percussion, vocals) / **High point:** "When You Find Out Who You Are" / **Discography in
August 1969:** *The Incredible String Band* (1966) / *The 5000 Spirits or the Layers of the Onion*
(1967) / *The Hangman's Beautiful Daughter* (1968) / *Wee Tam and the Big Huge* (1968)

"I'm Her Man" / "Going Up the Country" / "A Change Is Gonna Come" / "Turpentine Moan" / "Leaving This Town" / "Too Many Drivers" (Big Bill Broonzy) / "Rollin' Blues" (John Lee Hooker) / "Woodstock Boogie" / "On the Road Again"

CANNED HEAT

Saturday
7:30 p.m.
60 minutes

THE GROUP

Bob "The Bear" Hite (vocals, harmonica) / **Alan "Blind Owl" Wilson** (guitar, harmonica, vocals) / **Harvey "The Snake" Mandel** (guitar) / **Larry "The Mole" Taylor** (bass guitar) / **Adolfo "Fito" de la Parra** (drums) / **High point:** "On the Road Again" / **Discography in August 1969:** *Canned Heat* (1967) / *Boogie with Canned Heat* (1968) / *Living the Blues* (1968) / *Hallelujah* (1969)

…louds darkened the sky, and Canned Heat arrived …n stage at around 7:30 p.m. After the psychedelic …mblings of The Incredible String Band, the …udience was ready for a return to roots. Canned …eat managed to combine roots and blues with …opular success, a formidable blend that set the …Voodstock stage on fire.

At the end of July, the Californian blues group Canned Heat had played a… the Fillmore West in San Francisco. Henry "The Sunflower" Vestine lef… the group following a disagreement with the bass player, Larry "The Mole… Taylor. Two guitarists who were friends of the group replaced the deserte… at short notice: Mike Bloomfield, who had, notably, played with Bob Dyla… and Paul Butterfield, played in the first set; Harvey Mandel, who had th… excellent solo album *Cristo Redentor* to his name, took care of the second… Mandel then joined the group and, four or five concerts later, ended u… on stage with them at Woodstock. It must have been hard for the group… to get used to a new soloist; however, Mandel fitted in perfectly and the… year he spent with Canned Heat was the group's most interesting period… He left to join John Mayall (Keef Hartley's former boss) and subsequently… recorded with The Rolling Stones as a replacement for Mick Taylor (als… formerly with Mayall) before finally being replaced by Ron Wood. Ala… Wilson, the group's founder and its most distinctive voice, was about t… enter the last year of his life. He commited suicide on September 3, 1970… ten days before the death of Jimi Hendrix and a month before that of Jani… Joplin. All three were 27 years old. Thus, this Canned Heat lineup existe… for only a year, which began with Woodstock and included the super… album made with John Lee Hooker, *Hooker 'n Heat*.

CANNED HEAT

The group's members were first and foremost blues experts, and at th… time 78 r.p.m. records were not as widely available and information wa… not as readily accessible as today. However, they were in tune with th… times and brought their blues up to date by introducing unexpecte… instruments, such as a flute in "Going Up the Country" and a tambura… (a classical Indian instrument) in "On the Road Again."

Canned Heat played "Going Up the Country" second in their set, thu… getting the attention of the audience, who had already heard the son…

Opposite: The original lineup of Canned Heat included the guitarist Henry Vestine, who quit a few days before the festival. From top: Alan "Blind Owl" Wilson, Henry "The Sunflower" Vestine, Adolfo "Fito" de la Parra, Larry "The Mole" Taylor, and Bob "The Bear" Hite.

on the radio. From then on, the group could afford to dip into its more traditional repertoire for the rest of the set, and even to take it easy on stage with "Woodstock Boogie," a half-hour jam in which Adolfo de la Para regaled the audience with a drum solo that was both simple and highly musical. After this lesson in group improvisation, they came back on stage for an encore, "On the Road Again," which lasts just 3 minutes 30 seconds on the album but was extended to 10 minutes without falling into tedious repetition.

THE OWL, THE SNAKE, AND THE BEAR

Most of the groups playing at the festival had a clearly identifiable leader; however, Canned Heat was headed by three frontmen, each of whom contributed a particular quality to the ensemble. Alan Wilson was the total antithesis of the guitar hero as embodied at Woodstock by Santana, Leslie West, Johnny Winter, and Jimi Hendrix. When he sang, it was a thin, monotonous falsetto that skipped over the notes instead of a big, guttural voice. When he played, his solos took shape spontaneously, fitting his own rhythm, which was even more solid than that of the already deep groove of the group's rhythm section. And when he stressed certain notes, it was in the service of the overall musical idea. There were no piercing or strident notes, no outrageous vibrato, no pick (he played with his fingers), and no trace of ego.

In contrast, Harvey Mandel was the 1969 guitarist par excellence—shirt unbuttoned, large-headstock Fender Stratocaster. He used a fuzz pedal, controlled his sustain until it became feedback because of the volume, and he could have lapsed into cliché if his playing had not been profoundly original. He completely deserved his nickname of "The Snake," so much did his melodies weave in and out as they glided from one note to the next, following paths unknown to ordinary guitarists. The best part, of course, was the interplay between Mandel and Wilson. One would end the phrases played by the other, contradict him, ask him a question, or add a comment.

Bob Hite perfected this already sublime musical sculpture by adding a few plaintive harmonica notes, as muddy as the Mississippi, soft and rounded as one imagined the personality of this giant nicknamed "The Bear." It was his big voice that attacked the opening of "A Change Is Gonna Come" as if he wanted to preach its message. An incident in the middle of this song summed up the most glorious aspect of the Woodstock festival. A fan climbed up on stage and began to dance with Bob Hite, and a member of the security staff came up to make the young man get back down. But The Bear dismissed the security guard with a firm push of his paw; during Wilson's solo, Hite even offered a cigarette to the youth, who then returned to the audience. Add to this scene the gathering dusk and you have the makings of an instant, lasting legend. Thanks to this memorable performance, Canned Heat became, overnight, one of the greatest American blues groups.

HALLELUJAH

SETLIST

"Blood of the Sun" / "Stormy Monday" (T-Bone Walker) /
"Theme for an Imaginary Western" (Jack Bruce) / "Long Red" /
"Who Am I But You and the Sun" / "Beside the Sea" / "Waiting to
Take You Away" / "Dreams of Milk and Honey" / "Guitar Solo" /
"Blind Man" / "Dirty Shoes Blues" / "Southbound Train"

MOUNTAIN

Saturday
9:00 p.m.
60 minutes

THE GROUP

Leslie West (guitar, vocals) / **Felix Pappalardi** (bass guitar, vocals) /
Steve Knight (organ) / **Norman D. Smart** (drums) / **High point:** "Theme for
an Imaginary Western" / **Discography in August 1969:** *Mountain* (Leslie West's
solo album, 1969)

just like Santana, Mountain was one of those groups that began its career on the Woodstock stage, but that of the former would last many years, whereas Mountain would break up in 1972 under the strain of the group's various egos. Several solo careers, and regular reunions, would follow.

O riginally, the group developed from the solo work of the guitarist and singer Leslie West. He had started out with a New York garage rock band The Vagrants, some of whose recordings were produced by a man who was beginning to make a name for himself after having struggled in the small world of Greenwich Village: Felix Pappalardi. The two met when West made his first solo album in 1969, for which Pappalardi played bass guitar and keyboards as well as produced, and Norman D. Smart played drums. Putting it another way, three-quarters of the lineup that appeared at Woodstock under the name Mountain were on the album, which was entitled *Mountain*, while not actually being an album by Mountain. Four songs from the album featured on the setlist that evening.

THE CREAM OF THE BASS PLAYERS

Pappalardi did not come from obscurity; before producing West's album he worked on numerous others for Atlantic Records, most notably on the legendary Cream album *Disraeli Gears*. This 1967 classic owes a lot to Pappalardi—to the point that he has often been described as the group's fourth member. Not only was he producer for a trio that was notoriously hard to manage (Cream survived only another year after the album) but he took care of the arrangements and wrote the classic "Strange Brew" with his wife, Gail Collins. Mountain was a logical next step—a trio (supplemented by discreet keyboards) tasked with picking up the baton of heavy, virtuoso blues. The principle was the same: return to the influence of the great old-timers (hence the T-Bone Walker cover, the second song in Mountain's performance) and revive their music, adding heavy, exciting electrification, an intense, charged sound, and an instrumental approach that highlighted individual performances. Mountain could have been the new standard-bearer of heavy metal, if Led Zeppelin had not taken their

The trio behind
Mountain's huge sound:
Felix Pappalardi on
bass guitar, Norman
D. Smart on drums,
and Leslie West on
guitar and vocals.
Pappalardi played a
Gibson EB-1 bass. This
model, shaped like a
violin and launched in
1953, gave the German
manufacturer Hofner
the idea for the design
of its Violin Bass, which
would be popularized
by Paul McCartney.

AN IMAGINARY WESTERN AT YASGUR'S FARM

Unlike some other groups at Woodstock, whose lack of experience was
glaringly obvious, Mountain got by very well despite not having been
together long. Accounts vary, but this was either their third or fourth
concert. These musicians were not yet accustomed to playing together,
but they knew each other well enough for chemistry to happen. And they
were good—very good, even. From the start, with "Blood of the Sun," the
organ and guitar in unison were both impeccably put together and played
with obvious feeling. This magical combination endured throughout the
rest of the performance, centered on the gigantic personality of Leslie
West. After Canned Heat's The Bear, West was the festival's other
colossus—the group's name of Mountain was a reference to his physique.
In his hands, the Les Paul Junior guitar looked tiny, but he drew from it
an absolutely enormous sound that plenty of guitarists in possession of
far more expensive and celebrated instruments could only dream of. His
mastery of dynamics, with his finger permanently on the volume control,
was matched by his lyrical tone and impeccable choice of notes, including
in chord sequences that no longer had anything bluesy about them.
"Theme for an Imaginary Western," the superb song written by Jack Bruce,
was a magnificent example of this. Pappalardi sang the vocals, his thinner,
higher-pitched voice making a perfect counterpoint to West's thick, rocky
sound. This hour of perfect musical communion was the birth of a great
group, a moment so memorable for Mountain that, on their first album,
Climbing!, released in March 1970, the song "Who Am I But You and the
Sun" was retitled "For Yasgur's Farm."

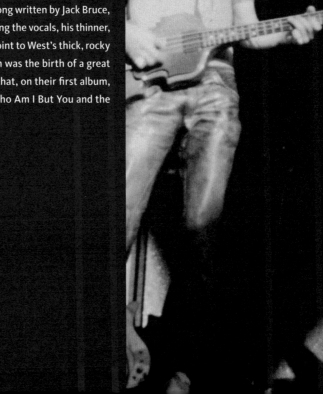

Saturday
10:30 p.m.
95 minutes

GRATEFUL DEAD

"St. Stephen" / "Mama Tried" (Merle Haggard) / "Dark Star" /
"High Time" / "Turn On Your Love Light" (Bobby Blue Bland)

Jerry Garcia (vocals, guitar) / **Bob Weir** (vocals, guitar) / **Phil Lesh** (bass guitar) /
Ron "Pigpen" McKernan (keyboards, harmonica, congas, vocals) / **Tom
Constanten** (keyboards, vocals) / **Mickey Hart** (drums) / **High point:** "Turn On
Your Love Light) / **Discography in August 1969:** *The Grateful Dead* (1967) /
Anthem of the Sun (1968) / *Aoxomoxoa* (1969)

The Grateful Dead's performance marked the start of the festival's biggest evening. The rest of the bill that Saturday consisted of only superstars—and among those superstars, no group possessed an aura comparable to that of the Dead in hippies' hearts. The arrival of these high priests of psychedelia promised a truly mystical experience.

GRATEFUL DEAD FROM THE MARS HOTEL

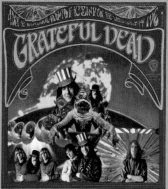

T he group from Palo Alto (a suburb of San Francisco, now famous for being home to the headquarters of Hewlett-Packard, Tesla, and Facebook) was far more than just musical entertainment for many. It was a state of mind in its own right, a community, and for many a way of life. From its beginnings the experience of hearing this group live went beyond the music and was profoundly connected to psychedelic drugs. The group's first concert under what was to be its permanent name took place on December 4, 1965, in California, during a famous Acid Test organized by the writer Ken Kesey. The aim of these events was simply to enable adventurous hippies to experience LSD under the best possible conditions, and the music of the Grateful Dead was already part of these experiences, which could make a trip even more powerful. The Dead embraced a concept of time that fitted perfectly with the effects of LSD: an extendable temporality that transported the listener into a trance, eased along by the repetitive quality of the rhythm section. The guitarist Bob Weir was a genius player, capable of maintaining an interesting rhythm on a single chord for far longer than many jazz musicians. Over this, the hippie icon Jerry Garcia, a shaggy teddy bear and the group's figurehead despite himself, developed solos that wove a web combining the blues of B.B. King, the country music of Merle Haggard, and the modal approach of John Coltrane. Improvisation was key to the point that some songs became excuses for a collective escape from reality. Consequently, no Grateful Dead concert was like any other, which is why the group's fans, a distinctive community known as the Deadheads, avidly collected official and unofficial recordings and followed the Dead caravan from one engagement to the next.

EQUIPMENT FAILURE

The Dead's Woodstock concert was also a unique experience that resembled no other concert by the group, but not always for the best. When a group leaves so much space for inspiration in the moment, there are bound to be

FOR
RENT

The weekend was great, but our set was terrible . . . We knew there were a half million people out there, but we couldn't see one of them.

Jerry Garcia

some evenings when it comes and others when it doesn't. Woodstock was one of the latter, but it was not purely the group's fault—they too suffered from technical issues. The group traveled with highly specialized, enormous equipment, and its sound system—which was largely the work of its sound engineer, Bear—made all the other groups jealous. However, the Woodstock stage was not ready to accommodate such a quantity of equipment and sagged under the weight of the huge system. To make matters worse, the stage was still damp, which made short circuits likely, and the quality of the power supply left much to be desired. The circuit was not properly earthed, and several ground loops occurred between the sound system and the amplifiers. When the musicians went up to the microphones, they got small electric shocks, which prevented them from concentrating and letting themselves go—the two prerequisites for successful improvisation. Given how the members were plagued by technical hassles, the group's performance was decent in the end. They played for only one-and-a-half hours, whereas its concerts often lasted more than two; however, in the setting of a festival this was not unusual.

RADIO INTERFERENCE

These failures were all the more frustrating in that the Dead at Woodstock should have been a landmark, one of those memorable gigs that would have fans swapping bootleg recordings with stars in their eyes, and which would have eventually been released as an album a few years later. No official recording of this live performance has ever been released. The aura of Woodstock was already conducive to the Dead being crowned as the leading lights of a movement capable of bringing together 500,000 people in a field in the middle of nowhere, and furthermore the Grateful Dead were enjoying their most fascinating period, a transition between their first psychedelic phase and their progression to country music. The group opened its set with "St. Stephen" from its latest album, *Aoxomoxoa*, and went straight on to "Mama Tried," a song by Merle Haggard. The choice of the two songs that opened the set could not have been more symbolic: the first typically psychedelic, the second a cover version of a country number. At the time, country music was that of "squares," of conservatism, which the hippie movement saw in a bad light. Indeed, that same year Haggard was to write in "Okie From Muskogee," "We don't smoke marijuana in Muskogee [a small town in Oklahoma]/We don't take trips on LSD". However, the Grateful Dead appropriated aspects of country music, turning it into a new source of inspiration. This set them apart from other psychedelic groups at the time.

Next, it launched into "High Time," but the group played for only the first 30 seconds before being interrupted by radio interference between its sound system and the organizational team's walkie-talkies. For 10 minutes, the group did not play and had a discussion, hoping that its technical team could fix the problem. In front of half a million people, and after only 7 minutes of music, 10 minutes is an eternity. But the group got back on its feet despite everything and, perhaps galvanized by this difficulty, began its performance proper. "Dark Star," one of those epic numbers that the Dead knew how to keep vibrantly thrilling at length, lasted almost 20 minutes, and the finale, "Turn On Your Love Light," a rhythm 'n' blues number, broke all records with a version that lasted some 40 minutes. Not bad for a concert that had been cut short.

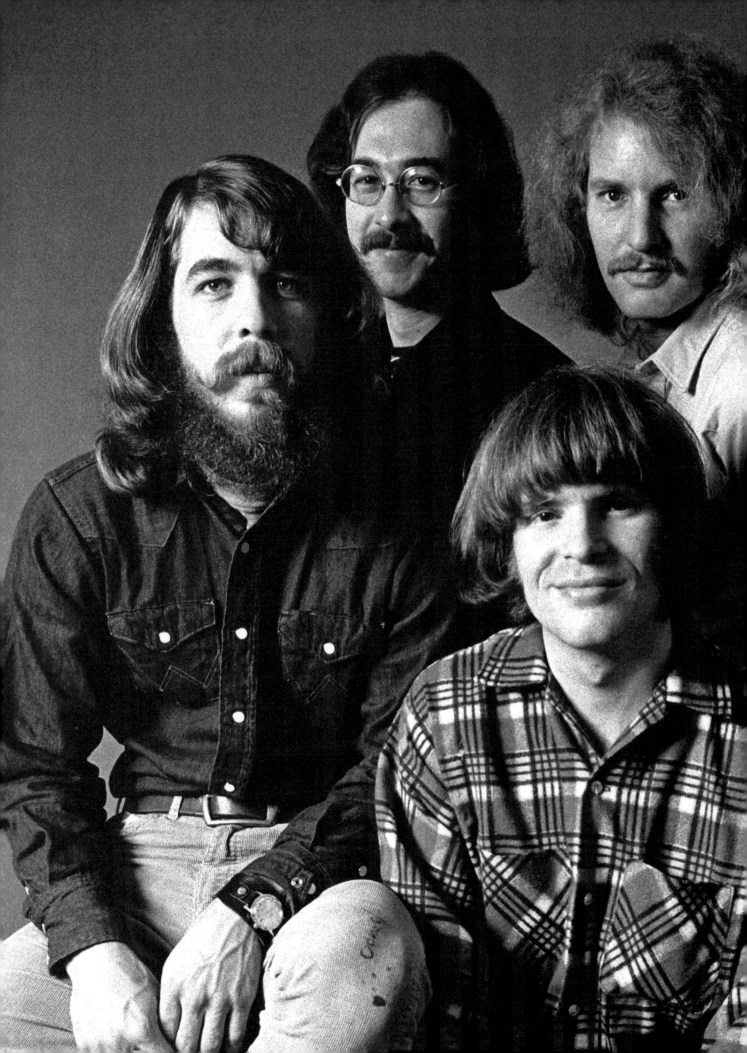

"Born on the Bayou" / "Green River" / "Ninety-Nine and a Half (Won't Do)" (Wilson Pickett) / "Bootleg" / "Commotion" / "Bad Moon Rising" / "Proud Mary" / "I Put a Spell on You" (Screamin' Jay Hawkins) / "Night Time Is the Right Time" (Roosevelt Sykes) / "Keep On Chooglin'" / "Susie Q" (Dale Hawkins)

CREEDENCE CLEARWATER REVIVAL

Sunday
12:30 a.m.
50 minutes

THE GROUP

John Fogerty (vocals, guitar, harmonica) / **Tom Fogerty** (guitar) / **Stu Cook** (bass guitar) / **Doug "Cosmo" Clifford** (drums) / **High point:** "I Put a Spell on You" / **Discography in August 1969:** *Creedence Clearwater Revival* (1968) / *Bayou Country* (1969) / *Green River* (1969)

ew groups were as symbolic of the year 1969 as Creedence Clearwater Revival, who marked the transition of the hippie generation toward harder rock. John Fogerty, the vocalist, lead guitarist, and leader of the group, complained about being scheduled after the Grateful Dead, who had supposedly sent their audience to sleep. In response, the group then played one of the most vigorous gigs in its short history.

Creedence Clearwater Revival's formation dated back to the end of the 1950s, and the group's four members spent the 1960s dividing their time between garage and rhythm 'n' blues. However, they started to record albums only in 1968, when John Fogerty and Stu Cook were discharged from all military service responsibilities after being reserves for two years. As soon as the group released its eponymous first album, things snowballed rapidly to the point that John Fogerty stayed with the group only until 1971, after six memorable albums. Creedence represented the spirit of 1969 perfectly; although they were a group, John's individuality made him the undisputed leader. The group played hits that were structured but also knew how to go off into extended solos and collective improvisation. It laid claim to the heritage of the bayou and the blues of the Deep South, but the musicians came from California. Creedence was sharper than the Grateful Dead and played better riffs than Jefferson Airplane, but they were less heavy and wild than Mountain. In 1969, the group took the charts by storm. Its album *Green River* had reached No. 1 and it had three consecutive hit singles: "Proud Mary," "Bad Moon Rising," and "Green River."

FATIGUE SETS IN

John Fogerty retains a vivid memory of the moment when he went on stage. He saw before him a great pile of naked bodies, grotesque and covered in mud—a scene he compared to Dante's *Inferno*. For a start, it was getting late (the music had begun at 12:30 p.m. and it was now 12:30 a.m.) and fatigue was setting in; furthermore, the Grateful Dead had just finished an improvisation lasting some 40 minutes and the audience did not seem especially eager to hear even more music. But truth can be discerned in adversity and John did not throw in the towel; on the contrary, he urged his group to make Creedence Clearwater Revival's performance more urgent and aggressive. This could be heard in his singing, which was ever

The Grateful Dead put half a million people to sleep and I had to go out and try to wake them up again.

John Fogerty

more hoarse than usual, and the music's tempo, which he unhesitatingly increased compared to that of the songs' original versions. What was lost in composure was gained in vigor and excitement.

The start did not bode well. Fogerty launched into the riff of "Born on the Bayou," and the rhythm section joined him in a train crash. The drums lost the beat, the rhythm guitar (played by John's brother Tom) took several notes to get started, and the bass guitar throbbed without finding its feet. Finally, everything fell into place when John began to sing, but doubts had already been sown. Was it because of the lack of monitor speakers that the group could not hear its own playing properly? Or because of a moment's hesitation faced with the sleeping human tide that greeted it? To try to overcome its difficult start, the group played hits without a break and without allowing Fogerty's solos to drag on too long.

Then came the cover of Screamin' Jay Hawkins' "I Put a Spell on You," which opened the group's first album. At that precise moment, it felt as if the musicians' playing was set free. The approach remained vigorous but softened slightly, just enough to regain that special groove that gave Creedence Clearwater Revival all their appeal. Fogarty's singing became more inspired, his solos more free. Was it the prospect of the gig coming to an end that gave the group back its lost energy? The fact remains that the finale of the performance was one of the high points of the evening, with a rendition of "Night Time Is the Right Time" performed as never before, and an extended harmonica solo in an epic version of the finale, "Susie Q." Doubtless a good many of the audience woke up at that point.

"Raise Your Hand" (Eddie Floyd) / "As Good as You've Been to This World" / "To Love Somebody" (Bee Gees) / "Summertime" (George Gershwin) / "Try (Just a Little Bit Harder)" (Lorraine Ellison) / "Kozmic Blues" / "Can't Turn You Loose" (Otis Redding) / "Work Me, Lord" / "Piece of My Heart" (Erma Franklin) / "Ball and Chain" (Big Mama Thornton)

JANIS JOPLIN

Sunday
2:00 a.m.
60 minutes

Janis Joplin (vocals) / **John Till** (guitar) / **Brad Campbell** (bass guitar) / **Richard Kermode** (organ) / **Maury Baker** (drums) / **Terry Clements** (saxophone) / **Cornelius "Snooky" Flowers** (saxophone) / **Luis Gasca** (trumpet) / **High point:** "Ball and Chain" / **Discography in August 1969** (with the group Big Brother & The Holding Company): *Big Brother & The Holding Company* (1967) / *Cheap Thrills* (1968)

The high priestess of psychedelic blues and queen of San Francisco, Texan Janis Joplin went on stage at 2:00 a.m., much later than originally scheduled, although it's impossible to tell at what time she should have played, as accounts differ. She waited her turn patiently, assisted by generous doses of psychoactive drugs.

At the age of only 26, Joplin had already lived several full lives, dividing her time between Texas and California, addicted to various substances and involved in relationships to varying degrees of toxicity. At the time of Woodstock, she was in a relationship with Peggy Caserta. The two of them arrived at the festival site in the same helicopter as Joan Baez. Caserta is often blamed for Joplin's drug use and addiction; in any event, Woodstock was no exception to her reckless drug use. Weary of waiting to go on stage, the only place where she could really be herself and feel at home, Janis turned to alcohol and heroin—a truly destructive cocktail. By the time she went on stage, at 2:00 a.m., the singer had plenty of time to get herself into an altered state, which could be seen from her conduct on stage, and heard in the way her voice began to fade quickly.

FROM ONE GROUP TO THE NEXT

This disappointing appearance was an even greater pity, because Janis was accompanied by a group that was much more in keeping with her musical vision than Big Brother & The Holding Company, who had been accompanying her since 1966. She had joined that group when she settled in San Francisco and became its frontwoman through force of circumstance. Her charisma and talent were too brilliant not to burst out beyond the confines of that little hippie quartet. When they performed at Monterey Pop Festival in June 1967, it was Joplin who was chosen to star in the poster of the December 1968 film, even though she was not one of the headliners: she had given a breathtaking performance. The members of the group produced an interesting sound, but it turned out they had technical limitations. After releasing two albums with them—one studio and one live—Joplin set up her own group, taking with her the most gifted guitarist of the bunch, Sam Andrew. With him, she recorded *I Got Dem Ol' Kozmic Blues Again Mama!* The album was released a month after Woodstock, but it had already been recorded by the time of the festival.

Sunday
3:30 a.m. 50 minutes

SLY & THE FAMILY STONE

SETLIST

"M'Lady" / "Sing a Simple Song" / "You Can Make It If You Try" /
"Everyday People" / "Dance to the Music" / "Higher/Music Lover" /
"I Want to Take You Higher" / "Love City" / "Stand!"

THE GROUP

Sly Stone (vocals, keyboards, harmonica) / **Freddie Stone** (guitar, vocals) /
Larry Graham (bass guitar) / **Rose Stone** (keyboards, vocals) / **Greg Errico**
(drums) / **Cynthia Robinson** (trumpet) / **High point:** "Higher/Music Lover" /
Discography in August 1969: *A Whole New Thing* (1967) / *Dance to the Music*
(1968) / *Life* (1968) / *Stand!* (1969)

You needed a great group led by an energetic, charismatic frontman to keep the audience awake in the dead of night—and no one could have managed it with as much panache as that group of wackos from San Francisco, Sly & The Family Stone. Many would have given up under such difficult conditions; instead, they played one of the festival's best gigs.

Until then, the festival's program had not stood out for its diversity; Richie Havens, who had opened the proceedings on the Friday, was the sole African American to have gone onto the Woodstock stage. (Subsequently, several festival organizers held what were known as "black Woodstocks," such as the Harlem Cultural Festival and Wattstax.) With the arrival of Sly & The Family Stone, a group that was a leading light of psychedelic funk rock and was already on its fourth album, the atmosphere changed totally, with a real mixed group, comprising different ethnicities and genders, and all coming together in music that was both highly energetic and experimental, kooky yet danceable.

The group's opening number was a festival in itself. The voices of its musicians blended, answered each other, harmonized, cried, and doubled the keyboard lines. The bass guitar purred under the expert fingers of Larry Graham; the guitars were sometimes raging, sometimes funky; and the brass punctuated the performance with perfectly placed interjections, avoiding ever lapsing into sterile displays. From a harmonic point of view, "M'Lady" is a simple song that uses just four chords, but Sly & The Family Stone turned it into a progressive epic worthy of Frank Zappa, without losing for a single second the incredible energy the group had at the start. They kept up that momentum, even increasing it in the excellent *a cappella* section that came just before a short organ solo, which said everything in a few notes. It is even disconcerting to listen to this intro now—and to think that it was recorded live at 3:30 a.m., before an audience of stoned or sleeping hippies.

PROBLEM? WHAT PROBLEM?

After the first song's perfectly placed finale, Sly Stone addressed the audience: "The problem is that, uh, we have some equipment . . . that is not working properly. So what we're gonna do is try to hurry up and play to avoid hanging you up or we can wait until the shit works right so that we

Opposite: Sly at his keyboard on stage at Madison Square Garden, New York, October 20, 1969—two months after Woodstock.

can play the way we'd like to." The group's performance of "M'Lady" was even more amazing in light of the fact that the musicians probably could not hear each other well while playing it. Indeed, a great rumbling sound could be heard behind Sly when he spoke, and his microphone fluctuated in volume for no apparent reason, as did Rose Stone's microphone, which she tested with a nonchalant "check, check." Unlike the Grateful Dead, Sly & The Family Stone did not allow themselves to be ruffled by technical hitches. A few seconds later, they launched into "Sing a Simple Song," one of the great numbers from their latest album, *Stand!* After the headlong rush of the first song, the group slowed the tempo but without losing energy—in fact, the opposite. The rhythm was so funky that it was impossible to listen to these five minutes of music without tapping your feet. Judging by the applause that greeted the end of the song, the audience seemed finally to have woken up.

The group managed to sustain this prodigious energy for the whole of the hour that followed—an achievement that was as marvelous as it was undreamed of. The true miracle of that night came in the middle of the medley "Higher/Music Lover," in which Sly Stone managed to get the audience to sing and shout. He showed colossal energy and resorted to a preacher's rhetoric to persuade everyone to join the party. "We're gonna try to do a singalong. A lot of people don't like to do it, because they feel that it might be old fashioned. But you must dig that it is not a fashion in the first place, it is a feeling, and if it was good in the past it's still good."

This historic gig was not to go unnoticed by the rest of the world, because Sly & The Family Stone were included in the movie *Woodstock*, thus exposing their music to a new audience, which earned unprecedented success for the albums they released in the early 1970s. And all the while struggling with faulty equipment.

"Heaven and Hell" / "I Can't Explain" / "It's a Boy" / "1921" / "Amazing Journey" / "Sparks" / "Eyesight to the Blind (The Hawker)" (Sonny Boy Williamson II) / "Christmas" / "Acid Queen" / "Pinball Wizard" / "Do You Think It's Alright?" / "Fiddle About" / "There's a Doctor" / "Go to the Mirror" / "Smash the Mirror" / "I'm Free" / "Tommy's Holiday Camp" / "We're Not Gonna Take It" / "See Me, Feel Me" / "Summertime Blues" (Eddie Cochran) / "Shakin' All Over" (Johnny Kidd & The Pirates) / "My Generation" / "Naked Eye"

THE WHO

Sunday
5:00 a.m.
65 minutes

 THE GROUP

Roger Daltrey (vocals) / **Pete Townshend** (guitar, vocals) / **John Entwistle** (bass guitar, vocals) / **Keith Moon** (drums) / **High point:** "Pinball Wizard" / **Discography in August 1969:** *My Generation* (1965) / *A Quick One* (1966) / *The Who Sell Out* (1967) / *Tommy* (1969)

To disturb one of Great Britain's biggest groups right in the middle of its rock opera, when its musicians were already irritated by having to wait hours before finally going on stage at 5:00 a.m., was probably not the greatest idea for putting forward a political viewpoint. And yet, that's what Abbie Hoffman did at Woodstock.

The Who was the biggest British group at Woodstock. The Beatles had not played live since 1966, The Rolling Stones opting to give a free concert in Hyde Park, and The Kinks had been barred from entry to the United States. So, of the top four, only The Who were at the top of the bill that second evening. Their album *Tommy* had been released in May, and it had already sold half a million copies—although it was a double album, and a concept album at that. With *Tommy*, The Who established rock music as a legitimate art form, and the album as a format that can tell a story from the first to the last song and uncoil a narrative thread through 24 vignettes, some of which could still become hit singles ("Pinball Wizard," of course). The term "rock opera" had not been invented for The Who, but the group exposed the medium to the wider public and would produce the two most popular examples of the genre. To drive the point home, instead of simply playing an incoherent string of hits, the musicians played the album almost in its entirety on stage, making their gig an artistic performance that extended the album experience. The appearance of The Who at Woodstock should therefore have been a perfect alignment of the planets, because it faced an audience open to conceptual concerts and happenings (such as the Grateful Dead), and hippies whose culture was not only musical but that also identified with Beat literature. But the group fell victim to the festival's poor organization as well as to the contradictions inherent in the movement, which exploded in the face of the assembled crowd at 5:30 a.m.

ACTIVISM

Before the first note had even been played, the gig got off to a bad start, because the group should have played much earlier, on Saturday evening, not in the small hours of Sunday morning. For a star act that had traveled from Great Britain, this treatment was difficult to accept, and it is easy to imagine the bitterness and anger felt by The Who when they were finally

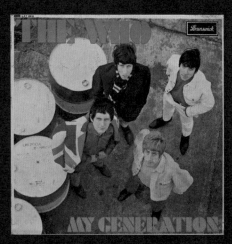

This superb shot captures the energy of The Who on stage at Woodstock. The guitarist Pete Townshend is kneeling down with his SG wearing a white boiler suit. On the left is the drummer, Keith Moon, with his two bass drums bearing the name Premier, which is a British brand.

plugged in and launched into "Heaven and Hell." This was a great group, and more than capable of playing with superb energy despite unideal conditions. Compared to the gigs they played at the Isle of Wight Festival (August 30, 1969) and Live At Leeds (February 14, 1970), both in England, the opening of this gig at Woodstock was a far cry from the enthusiasm of the other two. Despite everything, the group ran through its setlist, typical of the time, and embarked on *Tommy* with its third number.

Right in the middle of The Who's gig, just after "Pinball Wizard" and as the bass player, John Entwistle, was retuning his instrument, the activist Abbie Hoffman climbed on stage and grabbed the microphone Pete Townshend was using for his backing vocals. The founder of the Youth International Party (the "Yippies"), then began what was meant to be a political protest speech, "I think this is a pile of shit! While John Sinclair [one of the founders of the White Panthers] rots in prison . . ." But Townshend did not let him finish his diatribe, and reportedly ejected him from the stage with a blow from his guitar. "Fuck off my fucking stage. . . . The next fucking person who walks across this stage is gonna get fucking killed" before adding, a few seconds later, "You can laugh, but I mean it." At that moment, the entire hippie movement collapsed under the weight of its own contradictions, pulled in opposite directions by a taste for entertainment, its love of art, and the messages that art was supposed to convey.

But the group resumed right away with "Do You Think It's Alright?," the sole trace of Hoffman's appearance being the fact that Townshend's Gibson was completely out of tune following its use as a weapon. Then, like a carefully timed lucky coincidence, the sun rose to the sounds of "See Me, Feel Me," and the group delivered a truly luminous finale.

SETLIST

"The Other Side of This Life" (Fred Neil) / "Somebody to Love" (The Great Society) / "3/5 of a Mile In 10 Seconds" / "Won't You Try/Saturday Afternoon" / "Eskimo Blue Day" / "Plastic Fantastic Lover" / "Wooden Ships" (Crosby, Stills & Nash) / "Uncle Sam Blues" (Hot Tuna) / "Volunteers" / "The Ballad of You & Me & Pooneil" / "Come Back Baby" (Walter Davis) / "White Rabbit" / "The House at Pooneil Corners"

JEFFERSON AIRPLANE

Sunday
8:00 a.m.
100 minutes

THE GROUP

Grace Slick (vocals, tambourine) / **Marty Balin** (vocals, tambourine) / **Paul Kantner** (guitar, vocals) / **Jorma Kaukonen** (guitar, vocals) / **Jack Casady** (bass guitar) / **Nicky Hopkins** (piano) / **Spencer Dryden** (drums) / **High point:** "Volunteers" / **Discography in August 1969:** *Jefferson Airplane Takes Off* (1966) / *Surrealistic Pillow* (1967) / *After Bathing at Baxter's* (1967) / *Crown of Creation* (1968) / *Bless Its Pointed Little Head* (1969)

Jefferson Airplane was the real star of Saturday—the ultimate psychedelic group and the one that had established the genre's definitive form. In the end, the musicians found themselves playing at sunrise, at 8:00 a.m. on Sunday, before an audience that was slowly waking up.

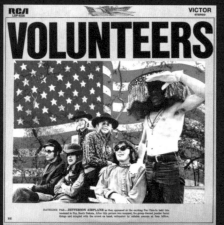

Grace Slick, the group's charismatic singer, set the tone at the outset: "Alright friends, you have seen the heavy groups, now you'll see morning maniac music."

Hard to be more hippie and psychedelic than Jefferson Airplane. Even the Grateful Dead did not sum up San Francisco and the famous Haight-Ashbury neighborhood to the same degree. It was okay for Deadheads to be hippies, but they were a separate community, and the music of the group they worshiped verged on country and modal jazz. Jefferson Airplane, on the other hand, started out under the specific influence of the Dead's Jerry Garcia (who is credited as the group's spiritual guide on their second album, *Surrealistic Pillow*), before making their sound more heavy and electric from *After Bathing At Baxter's*, in the ultimate synthesis of garage aggression and psychedelic strangeness. It has to be noted that the group was not short of talented musicians—far from it. On vocals, there were no fewer than three people: Grace Slick, Marty Balin, and Peter Kantner—the last of these also an outstanding songwriter who wrote, for example, "Wooden Ships" with Crosby and Stills. Jorma Kaukonen was on guitar, bringing a great variety of color to the group's music, thanks to his wealth of experience of acoustic blues. Finally, Jack Casady was on bass guitar, an instrument whose sound he modified through the use of several amplifiers that he designed himself.

A ROYAL GUEST

Jefferson Airplane managed to enjoy a certain amount of commercial success with music that was rather challenging—an extremely difficult balance to achieve. The group captured the spirit of the time and made music out of it. Only a week before their performance, on August 10, the musicians gave a free concert in Central Park, New York, proof of the magnitude of the phenomenon they represented had reached.

With three vocalists,
Jefferson Airplane
had an unusual
lineup. From left:
Paul Kantner, Grace
Slick, Spencer Dryden,
Marty Balin, and Jack
Casady. The guitarist
Jorma Kaukonen and
keyboard player Nicky
Hopkins do not appear
in this shot. Kantner
is holding a 12-string
Rickenbacker, an
instrument typical
in psychedelic music.

In spite of Woodstock's unpredictable schedule, Jefferson Airplane
went on stage and launched straight into "The Other Side of This Life," an
explosive cover of a song by the folk singer Fred Neil. From the first notes,
the group's cohesion was obvious. It had a shared energy, and it was clear
that the musicians were accustomed to playing under technical conditions
similar to those at Woodstock. They then came out with their biggest hit,
"Somebody to Love," and followed with relatively short songs leading up
to the main offering, the superb "Wooden Ships." This same song would
incidentally make a reappearance a few hours later, in the set played by
Crosby, Stills, Nash & Young, but in a radically different version. The one
by Jefferson Airplane stretched out for longer than 20 minutes—a mind-
blowing, profound piece of music.

Slick then introduced a guest who had arrived to join the group: Nicky
Hopkins. This British pianist had played with The Rolling Stones and The
Kinks, therefore becoming a representative of those groups who had not
made the trip across the Atlantic. He joined the group in "Volunteers,"

a song from its next album that had not yet been released but that had already been recorded, with Hopkins making a guest appearance. In his presence, the group made this antiwar hymn truly transcendent, producing an incredible performance of this song that the public was not yet familiar with.

"The Ballad of You & Me & Pooneil" was truly the climax of this gig, a journey lasting a quarter of an hour, pausing for a memorable bass guitar solo. (Incidentally, it was the festival's only moment of glory for this fairly recent instrument, which was invented in 1950.) The show came to an end shortly before 10:00 a.m. The few brave souls who had stayed up all night could finally go to sleep, because the next artist due on stage was scheduled for 2:00 p.m.

A

SUNDAY,
UGUST 17,
1969

FROM SUNDAY 2:00 P.M.
TO MONDAY 9:00 A.M.

Joe Cocker (vocals) / **Henry McCullough** (guitar) / **Neil Hubbard** (guitar) / **Alan Spenner** (bass guitar) / **Chris Stainton** (organ, piano) / **Bruce Rowland** (drums) / **Bobby Torres** (congas) / **High point:** "With a Little Help from My Friends" / **Discography in August 1969:** *With a Little Help from My Friends* (1969)

Sunday
2:00 p.m.
85 minutes

JOE COCKER

SETLIST

"**Who Knows What Tomorrow May Bring**" (Traffic) / "**Forty Thousand Headmen**" (Traffic) / "**Dear Landlord**" (Bob Dylan) / "**Something's Coming On**" / "**Do I Still Figure in Your Life**" / "**Feelin' Alright**" (Traffic) / "**Just Like a Woman**" (Bob Dylan) / "**Let's Go Get Stoned**" (The Coasters) / "**I Don't Need No Doctor**" (Ray Charles) / "**I Shall Be Released**" (Bob Dylan) / "**Hitchcock Railway**" (Dunn & McCashen) / "**Something to Say**" / "**With a Little Help from My Friends**" (The Beatles)

The person who opened Woodstock's last day was very much an unknown. But Joe Cocker's talent was so clear from his performance that it did not take long for him to conquer the audience and become an instant global star. He had it all: the look, the voice, the attitude, and a group that was willing to follow him.

I t's a reasonable assumption that, except for a few music connoisseurs in the know, no one at Woodstock had heard of Joe Cocker. His group, The Grease Band, came on stage first and played two instrumental numbers, much in the same way as Booker T. & The M.G.'s did at the Monterey festival before Otis Redding joined them. The two pieces were cover versions of Traffic songs, a nod to the man who had created the ideal blend of rock and soul—Steve Winwood.

JOE SHOWS UP

When Joe Cocker arrived on stage, he began by addressing the audience in an almost self-effacing way, "Yes, yes, well, good afternoon. . . ." Then he began playing, and no one could believe their eyes. Torn clothing, greasy hair, and dirty sideburns—this group's frontman looked as if he had been picked at random from the crowd of hippies. Unlike Roger Daltrey and Grace Slick, who had played the previous night, he was one of them, like a junkyard dealer singing for his work pals after a hard day's work. His flamboyance lay elsewhere: in his otherworldly voice. The raw, warm, rough sounds that emerged from his throat became nuggets of soul that instantly made him Britain's best answer to Ray Charles.

Needless to say, the performance was a visual one, too. Some frontmen hide behind their guitar; others execute dance steps to make their performance more appealing. But Cocker went beyond all that. The music transported him to the point that his whole body became a medium for expressing it, his passion clearly manifested through his spasmodic quivering and clenched hands. Half romantic madman, half possessed preacher, at Woodstock Cocker invented a new way of being a frontman. Like the obscene movements of Elvis 15 years earlier, his attitude was not rehearsed or intellectualized—it was just the music flowing through him and carrying him away.

It was just mind-blowing, totally turned the song into a soul anthem.

Paul McCartney

WITH A LITTLE HELP

Cocker began his set with a cover version of a song by the man who should have been there: Bob Dylan. "Dear Landlord" was from *John Wesley Harding*, a 1967 acoustic album. The Grease Band transformed the song into rock saturated with passion by adding two quiet passages that did not, however, cause the song to lose any tension. From the start, the audience held its breath. Cocker ended the set with the song that had given its name to his only album at that time: *With a Little Help from My Friends*. Originally a light number aimed at giving Ringo's voice some space on The Beatles' masterpiece, *Sgt. Pepper's Lonely Hearts Club Band*, this song was transformed into a masterly piece of mystical soul. This slowed-down version is the perfect example of a cover version that works. What might have been a mere footnote in the history of The Beatles became a classic for Cocker. This song is often cited as one of the most memorable moments of the entire festival—and with good reason.

There is no more of a thankless task than that of replacing the star everyone has come to see. Not only were Country Joe & The Fish asked to play in place of Jethro Tull, they also went on stage after a hellish storm, to face a distracted audience. Few artists would have dared to take up such a challenge.

Big black clouds had started gathering during Joe Cocker's performance, and a torrential downpour was unleashed on the audience at the final chord of "With a Little Help from My Friends." The festival was then transformed into a gigantic mudfest. Most of the hippies enjoyed this unexpected turn of events, indulging in sliding competitions, but the organizers were worried that the rain would cause members of the audience to be electrocuted. By some miracle, there were no accidents, and Country Joe & The Fish went on stage two hours late.

The bulk of the performance consisted of short numbers played by the excellent Barry Melton, aka "The Fish"—the group's psychedelic virtuoso. However, the audience needed more than that to make up for the loss of an incredible musical moment that had had to be canceled because of the rain—Ray Manzarek (The Doors' keyboard player) was supposed to jam with the Grateful Dead, but this performance became one of the great losses of the history of rock.

"Rock & Soul Music" / "(Thing Called) Love" / "Not So Sweet Martha Lorraine" / "Sing, Sing, Sing" / "Summer Dresses" / "Friend, Lover, Woman, Wife" (O. C. Smith) / "Silver and Gold" / "Maria" / "Love Machine" / "Ever Since You Told Me That You Love Me (I'm a Nut)" (Tiny Tim) / "Short Jam" (instrumental) / "Crystal Blues" / "Rock & Soul Music" (reprise) / the "FISH" cheer / "I-Feel-Like-I'm-Fixin'-to-Die Rag"

COUNTRY JOE & THE FISH

**Sunday
6:30 p.m.**
80 minutes

THE GROUP

"Country" Joe McDonald (guitar, vocals) / Barry "The Fish" Melton (guitar, vocals) / Doug Metzler (bass guitar) / Mark Kapner (organ) / Greg "Duke" Dewey (drums) / High point: The "FISH" cheer / Discography in August 1969: *Electric Music for the Mind and Body* (1967) / *I-Feel-Like-I'm-Fixin'-to-Die* (1967) / *Together* (1968) / *Here We Are Again* (1969)

"Spoonful" (Willie Dixon) / **"Good Morning Little Schoolgirl"** (Sonny Boy Williamson I) / **"The Hobbit"** / **"I Can't Keep from Crying Sometimes"** (The Blues Project) / **"Help Me"** (Sonny Boy Williamson I) / **"I'm Going Home"**

Sunday
8:15 p.m.
60 minutes

TEN YEARS AFTER

THE GROUP

Alvin Lee (guitar, vocals) / **Leo Lyons** (bass guitar) / **Chick Churchill** (organ) / **Ric Lee** (drums) / **High point:** "I'm Going Home" / **Discography in August 1969:** *Ten Years After* (1967) / *Stonedhenge* (1969) / *Ssssh* (1969)

As night fell, a British group that had been attracting the attention of crowds all over the United States went on stage at Woodstock. The musicians in Ten Years After were not yet stars, but the group had been championing its electric blues in the country since the summer of 1968 to increasingly large audiences.

T he group was part of the second wave of the British Invasion, following in the footsteps of The Yardbirds and The Rolling Stones. It was, of course, heavily influenced by Cream, which made Eric Clapton's absence from Woodstock all the more obvious. During this period, Alvin Lee was as much a circus freak as an acclaimed musician. He was nicknamed "the fastest guitarist in the West," because he could play blues riffs at high speed—something that was unheard of and exciting at the time.

STUDENTS OF THE BLUES

Of the six numbers the group played that evening, only two of them were originals. The rest were masterpieces of the Chicago blues style, written by the harmonica genius Sonny Boy Williamson I ("Good Morning Little Schoolgirl" and "Help Me") or the extraordinary double bass player Willie Dixon. "I Can't Keep from Crying Sometimes" was borrowed from a more recent source, the 1966 album *Projections* by the American group The Blues Project. By a curious coincidence, two of that group's members, Al Kooper and Steve Katz, were the founders of Blood, Sweat & Tears, one of the groups the was also on the festival's bill, and it was scheduled to appear just a few hours later.

The two original numbers that they played were largely excuses for collective or individual improvisation. "The Hobbit" was a drum solo by Ric Lee, while the 10-minute jam "I'm Going Home" highlighted Alvin Lee's incredible skill.

MOVIE STAR

His slim body, long blond hair, angel face, and heavily customized Gibson made Alvin Lee an instant icon. Michael Wadleigh, who made the movie *Woodstock* in 1970, certainly thought so, because he chose to include the song "I'm Going Home" in its entirety, focusing almost exclusively on Alvin Lee. This performance completely changed the group's reputation, making

A youthful-looking Ten Years After, with the four members who would remain together until 2004, despite two prolonged breaks. Behind, from left: Alvin Lee and Chick Churchill. Front: Leo Lyons and Ric Lee.

Ten Years After capable of filling an auditorium with 15,000 people. However, music aficionados know well that the best performance of the set was not "I'm Going Home" but "I Can't Keep from Crying Sometimes," a harrowing slow blues number. Had that song been chosen for the movie, Alvin Lee could have become a guitar hero of the likes of Beck and Clapton instead of "Captain Speed Fingers".

THE BAND

Sunday
10:00 p.m.
50 minutes

SETLIST

"Chest Fever" / "Baby Don't You Do It" (Marvin Gaye) / "Tears of Rage" / "We Can Talk" / "Long Black Veil" (Lefty Frizzell) / "Don't Ya Tell Henry" (Bob Dylan & The Band) / "Ain't No More Cane on the Brazos" (traditional) / "This Wheel's on Fire" (Bob Dylan & The Band) / "I Shall Be Released" (Bob Dylan) / "The Weight" / "Loving You Is Sweeter Than Ever" (The Four Tops)

THE GROUP

Robbie Robertson (guitar, vocals) / Rick Danko (bass guitar, vocals) / Garth Hudson (organ, piano, synthesizer) / Richard Manuel (organ, piano, vocals) / Levon Helm (drums, vocals, mandolin) / High point: "The Weight" / Discography in August 1969: *Music From Big Pink* (1968)

After a two-pronged British assault by Joe Cocker and Ten Years After, The Band marked the return to American music in its most traditional form. Although four of The Band's five members were, in fact, Canadian, the group was known for bringing folk music up to date.

G reenwich Village in the early 1960s had shaped folk into a solo art form, but The Band were a reminder that the rural musical traditions of 1930s America had been a collective activity, a social glue that forged the identity of the Southern countryside. In The Band, the individual was only an element of the bigger whole, a citizen in a democratic republic. Even the name—"The Band"—laid down this principle with the greatest simplicity and without placing any individual in the spotlight; each existed only through his contribution to the ensemble. This was at odds with the general tendency at the festival, which was to see a group as a jewelry box whose role was to let a diamond shine, whether it was a soloist (Alvin Lee in Ten Years After), a singer (Janis Joplin with Big Brother & The Holding Company), or both (Jimi Hendrix with Gypsy Sun & Rainbows). In their philosophy, The Band was much closer to the hippie ideals that had brought together a large proportion of the audience: everyone sang, and each put their voice and various instrumental talents to the service of the song as a community.

WHOSE BAND?

The group may have released only one album at the time it appeared, but The Band were nonetheless the oldest group at the festival. The group had existed in one form or another since 1958, when Levon Helm accompanied the rockabilly singer Ronnie Hawkins. The latter moved from Arkansas to Ontario, Canada, where he acquired the habit of poaching the best musicians from competing groups for his own, The Hawks. It was with him that the future The Band cut their teeth, developing a group sound and an unstoppable synergy over the course of countless gigs in bars and theaters all over Canada.

In 1963, the vocalist and his group went their separate ways, and then Bob Dylan got his hands on it. The group accompanied his 1965 tour—his first electric one, which provoked the wrath of some acoustic purists. It

Opposite: The Band pose in the woods near their Woodstock house, Big Pink, around the car belonging to the bass player Rick Danko. From left: Rick Danko, Levon Helm, Robbie Robertson, Richard Manuel, and Garth Hudson.

When we went up to Woodstock, we stopped listening to music for a year.

Levon Helm

was during this period that Dylan, with characteristic humor, decided to christen the group The Band.

In 1966, Dylan had a motorcycle accident, following which he withdrew from the public eye. He stopped touring and did not do so again until the mid-1970s. In the meantime, he settled in upstate New York in West Saugerties, six miles or so from the town of Woodstock. There, he played with The Band every day in the basement of a large pink house. The artists revisited traditional folk songs just for the fun of playing without any particular aim of recording them. These laid-back sessions would initially appear in the shape of the first bootleg recording in the history of rock—*Great White Wonder*—in July 1969, before being released officially as *The Basement Tapes* in 1975.

It was in that same house that The Band developed their repertoire as an independent group, and it was there, too, that they recorded *Music From Big Pink* in 1968. This album was huge, because it became the beacon for musicians who had reached the limit of psychedelia and were in search of a lost authenticity. The shift toward folk music made by George Harrison and Eric Clapton, for example, can be attributed entirely to The Band.

The group was therefore one of the most eagerly awaited groups at Woodstock. Their headquarters were some 60 miles from the festival site, and it would have been logical for Bob Dylan to join them on stage. For this reason, The Band's gig was the most obvious reminder of the festival's great absentee.

PERFECT HARMONY

The shadow of the great Zimmerman (a.k.a. Bob Dylan) can be discerned in the group's setlist, which revisited his song "I Shall Be Released" (in a sublime version, all subtlety and nuances) as well as two songs written with him: "This Wheel's on Fire" and "Don't Ya Tell Henry." However, The Band's talents extended well beyond the Dylan repertoire. The group also dipped into traditional folk songs ("Ain't No More Cane on the Brazos," "Long Black Veil") and into Motown rhythm 'n' blues ("Baby Don't You Do It," "Loving You Is Sweeter Than Ever"). Common to all of these was a group sound that was always alive, warm, and solid.

Garth Hudson opened the gig with a short, slightly hesitant organ solo. Then the other instruments joined him in the excellent "Chest Fever," and it became evident that, while no member of the group was a virtuoso soloist, no group sounded better together. Each note was in its place, in the space left by the notes the others didn't play. The blend of voices was impressive, especially for a live performance, and the way in which the timbres worked together—as when, coming out of a bridge passage, Levon Helm's gravelly voice responded to Richard Manuel's melancholic, thin voice—was a testament to the bond between the group's members.

"The Weight" was the true ending for the group's gig. This acoustic marvel was sung by Levon Helm, and the audience already knew it from the soundtrack of the movie *Easy Rider*, the definitive account of the death of the hippie dream that had been released a month earlier. The harmonies of Levon Helm and Rick Danko joyfully approached perfection, and when the whole group joined in for the chorus, it was impossible not to succumb. The Four Tops classic that followed, "Loving You Is Sweeter Than Ever," was more of a postscript, one final note of harmony before the impending storm of blues rock.

LIFE IN THE SLOW LANE
Members of The Band enjoy their Woodstock retreat at the house of Richard Manuel and Garth Hudson above Ashokan Reservoir. From left: Levon Helm, Robbie Robertson, Richard Manuel, Rick Danko, and Garth Hudson.

SETLIST

"**Mama Talk to Your Daughter**" (J. B. Lenoir) / "**Leland Mississippi Blues**" /
"**Mean Town Blues**" / "**You Done Lost Your Good Thing Now**" (Georgia
White) / "**Mean Mistreater Mama**" (Leroy Carr) / "**I Can't Stand It**" /
"**Tobacco Road**" (John D. Loudermilk) / "**Tell the Truth**" (The 5 Royales) /
"**Johnny B. Goode**" (Chuck Berry)

JOHNNY WINTER

Monday
12:00 a.m.
65 minutes

THE GROUP

Johnny Winter (guitar, vocals) / **Tommy Shannon** (bass guitar) / **Edgar Winter**
(organ, saxophone) / **"Uncle" John Turner** (drums) / **High point:** "Mean Town
Blues" / **Discography in August 1969:** *The Progressive Blues Experiment*
(1968) / *Johnny Winter* (1969)

After being lulled by The Band's perfect harmonies, the audience was unprepared for the electric storm that Johnny Winter was to bring. Not bothering with any kind of introduction, Winter launched straight in with two bars of guitar and vocals, with the rhythm section starting up immediately.

Ten Years After's efforts had been entirely worthy, but Winter was a phenomenon, a sublime anomaly. His guitar playing combined the mellowness of a B.B. King with the electric nerviness of a Muddy Waters, along with a Chuck Berry's feeling for riffs and the taste for improvisation on the edge of an abyss of a Jimi Hendrix. He was the perfect guitarist for an era that was starting to turn away from the jazzy experimentation of excessive psychedelia, and for an audience that sought the authenticity and simplicity of the blues, without abandoning the power of rock.

RIGHT PLACE, RIGHT TIME

Being so perfectly in tune with the times, Winter had already been accepted as one of the greats before Woodstock. Having been noticed by some decision-makers from Columbia Records at a concert in 1968, he had received the biggest advance ever paid to an artist at the time on signing a contract—the colossal sum of $600,000 (to put it in perspective, a record in those days cost $3). Columbia was doubtless gambling on Winter as the "perfect package," someone whose music spoke to rockers, bluesmen, and hippies—and whose flamboyant albino appearance made him into a phenomenon before he had even played a single note.

Winter perfectly represented the spirit of Woodstock, which the old guard of hippie groups handed over to the new generation of ruthlessly ambitious youngsters—virtuoso guitar heroes. His trio were not The Band: there was nothing rounded or mellow, it was angular and hard—even in a slow blues, such as "Mean Mistreater Mama," where the bass tone in itself was powerful. He was eagerly anticipated at the festival as one of the highlights of the third day, and was one of the few artists to be paid for his performance (a tidy sum of $3,750).

Opposite: The enthralling Johnny Winter poses with his superb Gibson Firebird V, the guitar he would be associated with all his life.

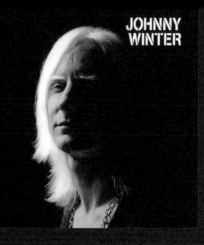

Johnny Winter in Amsterdam, April 26, 1970. The bass player behind him is Tommy Shannon, playing the white Jazz Bass that would become legendary when he was accompanying Stevie Ray Vaughan. Winter is playing an Epiphone Wilshire.

EXPLOSION

Of the nine songs that made up his performance, six were cover versions, but Winter made them his own as if they were part of his DNA. After opening with the explosive "Mama Talk to Your Daughter"—whose energy was far from the sedate, relaxed version by the acoustic bluesman J. B. Lenoir—Johnny segued without pausing for breath into "Leland Mississippi Blues," a slow blues whose heaviness would inspire the group Humble Pie, among others. The simplicity of the bass guitar/guitar/drums combination provided the space for solos, on which Winter never skimped. His virtuosity reached its peak in the third song, which he announced, "Some bottleneck guitar thing for you." There followed the gig's climax, the superb "Mean Town Blues," a rock number with riffs written by Winter that highlighted his slide guitar playing, which was to become his trademark.

Johnny then went without a break into two slow blues numbers before inviting his brother on stage. Edgar Winter, who was also an albino, was equally gifted, but his instrument of choice was the organ, with which he gave the trio's sound more substance as well as playing solos opposite Johnny. They launched into an excellent number that they had just recorded, "I Can't Stand It," which would become "I'm Not Sure" on the album *Second Winter*. "Tobacco Road" then gave Edgar the opportunity to switch from the organ to the saxophone before the finale brought together rhythm 'n' blues ("Tell the Truth") and rock 'n' roll ("Johnny B. Goode"), leaving the audience reeling in shock. The highly-anticipated performer had defended his position wonderfully, the only mistake being that of Winter's manager, Steve Paul, not agreeing for him to be featured in the movie of Woodstock. This decision cost him dearly, and left the way open for Alvin Lee to step into his shoes as blues rock virtuosi.

Still stunned by Johnny Winter's electrifying performance, the audience was less receptive to the soul jazz of Blood, Sweat & Tears. A gig in a muddy field at 1:30 a.m. on Monday, at a festival that was supposed to run from Friday to Sunday, was not the ideal setting to be introduced to their complex, cerebral music.

Blood, Sweat & Tears was the most jazzy group on the bill, with a complete, skilled brass section in the tradition of the rhythm 'n' blues albums of the time, but it had a pronounced taste for the more complex harmonies of New York jazz. The group that arrived at Woodstock was no longer the original Blood, Sweat & Tears, because the organist Al Kooper no longer sang with them and had been replaced by the Canadian David Clayton-Thomas.

Their eponymous second album, released in late 1968, was more pop and accessible than their first. It was a huge success, featuring no fewer than five hit singles and selling four million copies. It even won the Grammy Award for album of the year, beating The Beatles' *Abbey Road*.

MORE SWEAT THAN BLOOD

The saxophonist Fred Lipsius described the group's Woodstock gig as the worst of its career, and the only one in which Clayton-Thomas sang out of tune. The group was probably accustomed to better technical conditions, and the festival's folk music bias hardly motivated the musicians to give it their all. For the audience, too, the result must have been less accessible than the unequivocal assault of sound from the previous gig by Johnny Winter. The group performed "Something's Coming On," which had been sung only a few hours earlier by the person who wrote it, Joe Cocker. The comparison was unflattering for Clayton-Thomas, who was far from possessing the animal charisma of the rocker from Sheffield, England. Despite everything, the musicians performed a memorable version of the funk gem "Spinning Wheel"—perfect for opening the audience's ears to other worlds of sound while awaiting the arrival of the next act, the four heroes of the hippie movement.

BLOOD, SWEAT & TEARS

Monday
1:30 a.m.
60 minutes

BLOOD, SWEAT & TEARS
in 1971, from left: Steve Katz, Dick Halligan, David Clayton-Thomas, and Fred Lipsius.

CROSBY STILLS NASH & YOUNG

**Monday
3:00 a.m.**
60 minutes

THE GROUP

David Crosby (vocals, guitar) / **Stephen Stills** (vocals, guitar, organ, piano) /
Graham Nash (vocals, guitar, organ) / **Neil Young** (vocals, guitar, organ, piano) /
Greg Reeves (bass guitar) / **Dallas Taylor** (drums) / **High point:** "Suite: Judy
Blue Eyes" / **Discography in August 1969:** *Crosby, Stills & Nash* (1969)

SETLIST

Acoustic set: **"Suite: Judy Blue Eyes"** / **"Blackbird"** (The Beatles) /
"Helplessly Hoping" / **"Guinnevere"** / **"Marrakesh Express"** / **"4 + 20"** /
"Mr. Soul" (Buffalo Springfield) / **"I'm Wondering'"** / **"You Don't Have to Cry"**
Electric set: **"Pre-Road Downs"** / **"Long Time Gone"** / **"Bluebird
Revisited"** / **"Sea of Madness"** / **"Wooden Ships"** Acoustic encores:
"Find the Cost of Freedom" / **"49 Bye-Byes"**

Despite a rich setlist, the gig lasted only an hour. Crosby, Stills, Nash & Young knew how to serve up a song, but unlike most of the artists on the bill, they did not stretch out their songs with jams and solos. You could almost say that their egos were so enormous they no longer needed anyone's approval.

T he four musicians had not really had time to prepare for the gig. Their only public appearance together had been in Chicago the previous evening, on August 16, and it was a gig consisting of four songs—without Neil Young. So it is a safe bet that they chose songs they knew well, not having the time to take risks with their structure. The setlist included the whole of their first album, released three months earlier (without Neil Young), with the exception of "Lady of the Island." By an unfortunate coincidence, that was a love song addressed to Joni Mitchell, one of the festival's great absentees. But she was not completely forgotten, because "Guinnevere" addressed the same muse.

Graham Nash and David Crosby harmonize during Crosby, Stills, Nash & Young's electric set.

PERFECT HARMONY

The gig was split into three parts, each with a radically different atmosphere. It began with the original trio, Crosby, Stills & Nash, with no rhythm section and without Young. The atmosphere was relaxed, almost informal, like watching them rehearse in their living room. Stills did not hesitate to give the sound engineer instructions in between playing two lines, and he was heard requesting, "a little less bottom on the guitar please," probably to lighten a dull sound. Beyond the laid-back attitude, starting with "Suite: Judy Blue Eyes" provided a challenge, because it lasts more than 7 minutes and is divided into several parts. But Crosby, Stills & Nash tackled the task with ease, producing perfectly tuned vocal harmonies. Stills sang the lead part (he wrote the song) and played a 6-string acoustic guitar, while Crosby played a 12-string and harmonized with Nash. This arrangement came naturally; it was said that those three were truly well suited to each other.

THE CALM AND THE STORM

The song "4 + 20" was the only one from *Déjà vu*, the album they were recording at the time of the Woodstock gig, and that would be the first

It's the moment when all of that generation of hippies looked at each other and said, "Wait a minute, we're not a fringe element. There's millions of us!"

David Crosby

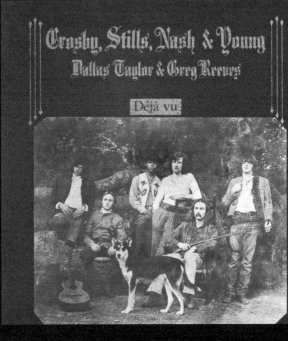

studio album with Young. However, the latter joined the trio for the next song, "Mr. Soul." This was one of the hits by the group Buffalo Springfield, in which Stills and Young both played. They played as a duo for the last three songs of the acoustic set.

Crosby, Nash, and the rhythm section then arrived on stage and set up for the electric part of the gig. The first two songs were from the first album, and were followed by two unreleased numbers: "Bluebird Revisited," which would eventually appear on Stills's second solo album in 1971 (*Stephen Stills 2*), and "Sea of Madness," which has never been released, apart from the version performed at Woodstock. The second set reached a peak with a magnificent rendition of "Wooden Ships," a real climax punctuated by more well-judged solos from Stills and Young. Finally, the original trio came back on stage for two acoustic encores, one of them the short "Find the Cost of Freedom"—another unreleased song, which would be included on the 1971 live album, *4 Way Street*.

Some of the performances at Woodstock deserved a live album in their own right, and this one gifted by four musicians at 3:00 a.m. was one of them. However, Neil Young did not feel that way, or so it is believed, as reportedly he refused to allow his name to appear in the movie or on the album—he had always been a difficult character to understand. The group that had to perform after CSNY had a hard act to follow.

HARMONY

The original trio opens the gig, playing acoustically. From left: David Crosby on the 12-string Martin, Graham Nash with his hands in his pockets, and Stephen Stills singing lead vocals in this song, playing a 6-string Martin with an open tuning. A total of 18 strings that created a cathedral of sound.

Monday
6:00 a.m.
70 minutes

THE PAUL BUTTERFIELD BLUES BAND

THE GROUP

Paul Butterfield (vocals, harmonica) / **Howard "Buzz" Feiten** (guitar) / **Rod Hicks** (bass guitar) / **Ted Harris** (organ) / **Phillip Wilson** (drums) / **Steve Madaio** (trumpet) / **Keith Johnson** (trumpet) / **David Sanborn** (saxophone) / **Trevor Lawrence** (saxophone) / **Gene Dinwiddie** (saxophone) / **High point:** "Driftin' Blues" / **Discography in August 1969:** *The Paul Butterfield Blues Band* (1965) / *East-West* (1966) / *The Resurrection of Pigboy Crabshaw* (1967) / *In My Own Dream* (1968) / *Keep On Moving* (1969)

Two hours after Crosby, Stills, Nash & Young had played their last notes, The Paul Butterfield Blues Band provided music for the sunrise that Monday, August 18. A large part of the audience had already left, but those who remained were there to listen to the superstar of the Chicago blues band. Instead, they were treated to a fine demonstration of jazzy blues tinged with rhythm 'n' blues.

Opposite: The Paul Butterfield Blues Band in 1967, from left and from top: Gene Dinwiddie (saxophone), Paul Butterfield (harmonica, vocals), Keith Johnson (trumpet), Elvin Bishop (guitar), Mark Naftalin (keyboards), Philip Wilson (drums), Bugsy Maugh (bass guitar), and David Sanborn (saxophone).

Paul Butterfield was one of a handful of youngsters born in Chicago during the 1940s who were blown away by a kind of music that shouldn't have been theirs. The explosion of Chicago blues on the Chess label, and of artists such as Muddy Waters and Howlin' Wolf, had for the most part left white audiences indifferent—until this music was taken up and adapted by British groups. But Butterfield did not wait for this rediscovery to happen, and he became a harmonica virtuoso in the great tradition of the Windy City. Gradually, he began to come across other white kids who loved this music, including the guitarist Elvin Bishop, with whom he formed The Paul Butterfield Blues Band. In 1964, the group recruited the incredible Michael Bloomfield who, although he spent barely a year as a member, revealed himself during that time to be one of the greatest electric blues guitarists. In 1965, The Paul Butterfield Blues Band was on the bill of the Newport Folk Festival. Bob Dylan heard their set and became one of the group's first fans, and he asked them to accompany him in three songs during his gig the following day—an electric decision that made history.

The Paul Butterfield Blues Band was a kind of American version of John Mayall's Bluesbreakers—a group formed around a frontman that would never make it big but whose musicians would enjoy fine careers elsewhere. Elvin Bishop would have solo hits, Bloomfield would go on to form The Electric Flag, and the saxophonist David Sanborn would record albums with James Brown, David Bowie, and Stevie Wonder.

HESITATION

Like the Bluesbreakers, The Paul Butterfield Blues Band were a musical weathercock, adapting the tone of their blues to suit the fashion of the moment. Their eponymous first album was a gem of pure electric blues, whereas *East-West* explored modal jazz and Indian classical music. The group that went on stage at Woodstock launched into a brass-heavy rhythm 'n' blues (the brass section numbered five musicians, making it

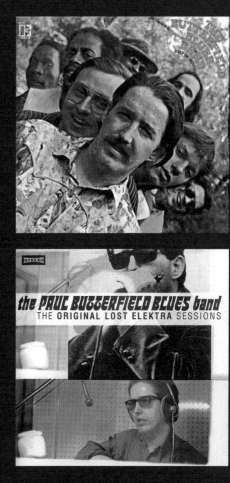

the festival's biggest), much more cerebral and rich in arrangements than it had been three years earlier. On guitar, Buzz Feiten had replaced Bishop, and this highly gifted young man (he was only 20 years old at the time of the gig) mastered to perfection the difference between roots blues and Blood, Sweat & Tears-style fusion imposed on him by Butterfield.

"No Amount of Loving" got lost in arrangements, but "Driftin' Blues" was a fine demonstration of what the group did best, with a majestic harmonica solo by the boss. "Love March" was an attempt at parodying a military march by giving it pacifist lyrics, over which Butterfield harangued the crowd, "If you wasn't so tired, you could all get up and just march around this whole area here." The number that followed would have been more in place in a Broadway musical. The group then finally redeemed itself with a superb finale, "Everything's Gonna Be Alright," in which Feiten soared over the brass lines with a simple, brilliant solo. The Paul Butterfield Blues Band was clearly equally capable of producing the best and the most questionable music, and it delivered both that morning to the audience at Woodstock—who still had some surprises in store.

Opposite: The group's lineup as heard on the album *East-West* (1966), during the shoot for the album sleeve: Billy Davenport (drums), Mark Naftalin (keyboards), Mike Bloomfield (guitar), Paul Butterfield (harmonica, vocals), Elvin Bishop (guitar), and Jerome Arnold (bass guitar).

Woodstock was not an exclusively psychedelic festival. On the bill, there were also some odd diachronic anomalies, such as Sha Na Na. No one had been waiting for them, however, their half-hour on stage launched a groundswell of significance.

S ha Na Na can probably boast that it performed at the most awkward time on the Woodstock bill: just before the finale played by Jimi Hendrix. To make matters worse, this unknown group that sprang from Columbia University's *a cappella* group played music that was already outdated at the time. Far from experimental distorted guitar sound and Indian fashions, this group of eight singers (accompanied by a small group of dancers) performed old-style rock—most of the songs they played dated from before 1960.

Caught between Paul Butterfield and Jimi Hendrix, Sha Na Na's music must have felt refreshing, with 12 numbers in 30 minutes, no solos lasting more than 12 bars, and some dancing on stage. The 1950s had the party spirit, and brevity, too—it was poles apart from the sometimes esoteric musical quests of 1969.

The group's inclusion in the *Woodstock* movie and compilation made it into a phenomenon, with constant tours and an eponymous TV show that was broadcast over four years. Beyond this individual success, it reminded America of its glorious past, before it was mired in Vietnam and the various moral crises of the 1960s—a wave of nostalgia encouraged by the musical *Grease*, the TV series *Happy Days*, and the movie *American Graffiti*. It just goes to show that sometimes it's smart to be different.

Monday
7:30 a.m.
30 minutes

SHA NA NA

SETLIST

"Get a Job" (The Silhouettes) / **"Come Go with Me"** (The Del-Vikings) / **"Silhouettes"** (The Rays) / **"Teen Angel"** (Mark Dinning) / **"Jailhouse Rock"** (Elvis Presley) / **"Wipe Out"** (The Surfaris) / **"Blue Moon"** (Billy Eckstine) / **"The Book of Love"** (The Monotones) / **"Little Darling"** (The Gladiolas) / **"At the Hop"** (Danny & The Juniors) / **"Duke of Earl"** (Gene Chandler) / **"Get a Job"** (reprise/The Silhouettes)

THE GROUP

Joe Witkin (vocals, keyboards) / **Donald "Donny" York** (vocals) / **Rob Leonard** (vocals) / **Alan Cooper** (vocals) / **Frederick "Dennis" Greene** (vocals) / **Dave Garrett** (vocals) / **Richard "Richie" Joffe** (vocals) / **Scott Powell** (vocals) / **Henry Gross** (guitar) / **Elliot "Gino" Cahn** (guitar) / **Bruce Clarke III** (bass guitar) / **Jocko Marcellino** (drums) / **High point:** "At the Hop" / **Discography in August 1969:** No albums

"Message to Love" / "Hear My Train A Comin'" / "Spanish Castle Magic" / "Red House" / "Mastermind" (Larry Lee) / "Lover Man" / "Foxey Lady" / "Jam Back at the House" / "Beginnings" / "Izabella" / "Gypsy Woman/Aware of Love" (The Impressions) / "Fire" / "Voodoo Child (Slight Return)" / "Stepping Stone" / "The Star-Spangled Banner" (John Stafford Smith) / "Purple Haze" / "Woodstock Improvisation" / "Villanova Junction" / "Hey Joe" (The Leaves)

Monday
9:00 a.m.
130 minutes

JIMI HENDRIX

THE GROUP

Jimi Hendrix (guitar, vocals) / **Billy Cox** (bass guitar) / **Mitch Mitchell** (drums) / **Larry Lee** (rhythm guitar) / **Juma Sultan** (congas) / **Gerardo "Jerry" Velez** (congas) / **High point:** "The Star-Spangled Banner" / **Discography in August 1969:** *Are You Experienced* (1967) / *Axis: Bold as Love* (1967) / *Electric Ladyland* (1968)

Jimi Hendrix was given the weighty task of bringing the Woodstock festival to a close, on Monday morning, before a scattered, totally exhausted crowd. When making the decision to have him play last, the organizers must have hoped for a performance of the caliber of two years earlier at the Monterey Pop Festival.

H owever, that legendary gig, which involved a guitar being burned (among other things), had taken place under entirely different circumstances. Hendrix had returned from England to show his native country what he was made of. He had everything to prove, all the more so because at Monterey he was performing before The Who, and he wanted to make it known that he was much more than an opening act.

At Woodstock, Hendrix had conquered his audience in advance, and he was awaited by the hippies as the mystical experience many of them hoped for. He already enjoyed a near-legendary reputation and no longer needed his band to attract a crowd—his name alone was enough. So he showed up at Woodstock with a new group, created for the occasion from the ruins of The Jimi Hendrix Experience trio, which had played its last gig on June 29 in Denver. Chip Monck had announced the concert as "The Jimi Hendrix Experience," but Hendrix corrected him diplomatically and briefly, saying, "We got tired of the Experience."

The group turned out to be a collection of old hands and newcomers. It included Mitch Mitchell, the Experience's drummer; Billy Cox on bass guitar, one of Hendrix's army friends who he had been jamming with since 1961; Larry Lee on guitar, an old friend of Hendrix and Cox who had returned from Vietnam just two weeks earlier; and the two percussionists Jerry Velez and Juma Sultan, who were still unknown at the time. This lineup, hastily assembled to honor the pre-existing commitment of Woodstock, had not had time to prepare ("We only had two rehearsals"), so their alchemy was nowhere near that of the trio that had preceded them. Indeed, on recordings of the Woodstock concert Larry Lee's guitar and the congas of Velez and Sultan are hardly audible, because they are completely undermixed.

Opposite: Hendrix in the morning light, his foot on the control pedal of his Uni-Vibe.

You can imagine how many bloody joints were smoked and God knows what else, and what other chemicals were inhaled in order to stay on top of it.

Eddie Kramer

HENDRIX'S INNER CONFLICT

Rumor has it that Hendrix had refused to play at midnight that night (so Johnny Winter then went on stage), preferring to wait until the end of the festival to bring it truly to a close, despite the delay. He then arrived on stage at 9:00 a.m. on Monday, although a large proportion of the audience had left during the night, leaving Hendrix to play to around one-tenth of the 400,000 people who had been present the previous evening. To make matters worse, of the diehards who had remained, not all waited for the end of the gig, and Hendrix, who had not slept since the start of the festival, ended his performance at 11:00 a.m. in front of a sparse audience.

"Message to Love," the number that opened the set, was still unreleased at the time, as were half of the songs performed. The setlist clearly conveyed Hendrix's inner conflict, between what was expected of him—that he play the Experience's hits and that he play with his teeth—and what he would have liked to do, which was to play new, more jazzy numbers and concentrate on music rather than spectacle. The setlist therefore included hits from *Are You Experienced*; just one number each from the Experience's two other albums (*Axis: Bold as Love* and *Electric Ladyland*); a song by Larry Lee, sung by him ("Mastermind"); two songs by The Impressions (the group led by Curtis Mayfield, one of Hendrix's idols) that Lee also sang; three instrumental jams ("Jam Back at the House," "Woodstock Improvisation," and "Villanova Junction"); and the aforementioned unreleased songs, which would appear on numerous posthumous albums but which Hendrix would never finish.

The sound was powerful but unpolished. Each member played their thing and the group lacked cohesion. Generally speaking, Hendrix played loudly and out of tune. Indeed, he warned the audience while tuning his guitar haphazardly before "Red House," "We don't wanna play too loud

for you, so we'll just play very quiet and very out of tune." He would keep only one of those promises, and the volume of the incessant attack of sound ended up being wearisome.

ANTHEM

The high point of his performance came when Hendrix, accompanied only by Mitch Mitchell's cymbals, launched into a psychedelic, impressionistic version of the American national anthem, the famous "The Star-Spangled Banner." He used an extremely broad palette of effects on his Stratocaster guitar, imitating bombs, machine guns, and the total chaos of war as a definitive summary of the situation of the United States in Vietnam. Few moments had captured and summed up the spirit of 1969 as well as those noisy 3 minutes of fragile beauty.

But the gig's real conclusion came in the final lyrics of the last number, the reprise of The Leaves' song "Hey Joe," the Experience's first single, released in 1966, with "Where you gonna run to now, where you gonna go?" The question was addressed both to Hendrix himself, who would spend the last year of his life (he died in September 1970) looking for his next musical direction, between *Band Of Gypsys* and the reformation of the Experience, but also, above all, to the audience, to the hippie generation who could not avoid the question of the meaning of their movement, beyond the symbol of an apparent coming together that Woodstock had been for those three days. Without realizing it, Hendrix brought the festival to a close in the most pertinent way possible.

EPILOGUE

Hendrix brought the festival to a close on Monday morning. Here, he is seen from behind, his red bandana as identifiable as his fringed white jacket, photographed from the green room next to members of the organizational team. Among them, a jacket adorned with the festival poster can be seen—a fine symbol of a happy ending.

Absentees

Everyday Life

The Guitars of Woodstock

Altamont

The Movie and Albums

Legacy

EPILOGUE

The Isle of Wight Festival of Music
Woodside Bay near Ryde——I.o.W

AUGUST 29★30★31st '69————— season ticket £2~10

Present
Bob Dylan
the band & ritchie havens

Free Concert 29th ———— to season ticket holders

the Who Moody Blues Fat Mattress Joe Cocker
Bonzo Dog Band Family Free Pretty Things
Marsha Hunt & White Trash Batterd Ornaments
Aynsley Dunbar Retaliation Blodwyn Pig Gipsy
Blonde on Blonde Edgar Broughton Band
King Crimson   25/-

Saturday 30th

Sunday 31st

Bob Dylan & The Band Ritchie Havens Tom Paxton
Pentage Julie Felix Gary Farr Liverpool Scene
Indo Jazz Fusions Third Ear Band   £2

BOB DYLAN

THE GROUP

Bob Dylan (vocals, guitar, piano)
Robbie Robertson (guitar, vocals)
Rick Danko (bass guitar, vocals)
Garth Hudson (organ, piano, synthesizer)
Richard Manuel (organ, piano, vocals)
Levon Helm (drums, vocals, mandolin)

SETLIST

With The Band: **"She Belongs to Me"** / **"I Threw It All Away"** / **"Maggie's Farm"**

Solo: **"Wild Mountain Thyme"** (Francis McPeake) / **"It Ain't Me Babe"** / **"To Ramona"** / **"Mr. Tambourine Man"**

With The Band: **"I Dreamed I Saw St. Augustine"** / **"Lay Lady Lay"** / **"Highway 61 Revisited"** / **"One Too Many Mornings"** / **"I Pity the Poor Immigrant"** / **"Like a Rolling Stone"** / **"I'll Be Your Baby Tonight"** / **"Quinn the Eskimo"** / **"Minstrel Boy"** / **"Rainy Day Women #12 & 35"**

Of all the artists who did not play at Woodstock, Bob Dylan is the one who left the biggest void, so much so that, 50 years on, some still have not gotten over it and continue to believe that the poet-singer from Duluth made the trip to Max Yasgur's farm.

He would have been more than welcome. Michael Lang was a big fan of Dylan, who single-handedly stood for the whole counterculture, and even, initially, saw the festival as a tribute to his work. Before his motorcycle accident, Dylan was caught between a rock and a hard place. On the one hand, the folk purists had not forgiven him for going electric, and on the other, his hero-worshipping fans saw in him a messiah whose every act and gesture warranted interpretation. He retreated from public life from 1967 to 1974, only performing live a handful of times, and he turned down the invitation to Woodstock because his son, Jesse, was ill. The illness was doubtless real, like Dylan's accident, but it is easy to imagine that it provided an excuse to politely decline participating in a concert that put him ill at ease.

The festival eventually took place at Bethel, which was geographically close to Dylan, and The Band's presence on the bill kept alive the hope that the singer might make an appearance, even by surprise, even in disguise and under a pseudonym. However, he was so far from taking part that he was already elsewhere, en route to England. He had embarked on August 15, the first day of Woodstock, and was on his way to performing one of only four concerts in his seven year retreat from the public eye, at the Isle of Wight festival. It is unclear why Dylan chose one festival over the other.

He appeared there with The Band, alternating between numbers with the group and solo songs with acoustic guitar. In light of his last two albums, the enigmatic *John Wesley Harding* (a gem of dark folk songs) and *Nashville Skyline* (a bizarre potpourri of country numbers), the audience did not know what kind of setlist to expect, all the more since Dylan already had a reputation for enjoying confusing his audience.

The opening was predictable with the classic "She Belongs to Me," the new song "I Threw It All Away" (one of three good songs on *Nashville Skyline*), and a reference to his turbulent past, "Maggie's Farm"—the song which he had opened with in his famous electric set at the Newport Festival in 1965. No "Masters of War," let alone "Blowin' in the Wind," and no songs from before 1965. Dylan had moved on and was encouraging his audience to do the same. On his return to the United States, he discovered to his horror that many of the hippies who had gone to the Woodstock festival had made a pilgrimage to his house, awaiting the return of Ulysses. He never appeared there, but Woodstock pursued Dylan.

LED
ZEPPELIN

As Woodstock symbolizes the handover from the groups of the 1960s to the avant-garde hard rock and heavy metal of the 1970s, it would have made sense for the most immense quartet of the latter decade to be at the party. It was discussed, but Led Zeppelin ended up choosing to perform at another concert.

Formed at the end of 1968, Led Zeppelin was a British group that soon became the must-see attraction for lovers of heavy, aggressive blues. Its guitarist Jimmy Page had already toured in the United States with The Yardbirds and, when he formed The New Yardbirds, he made sure he kept the manager who had organized the previous tours. When Led Zeppelin was ready, Peter Grant, the manager in question, only needed to renew existing contacts to organize an inaugural tour with great fanfare.

Led Zeppelin had released only their eponymous first album, but the group was already on its third American tour, which happened to pass through the East Coast during the summer of 1969. It would therefore have been easy for them to travel to Woodstock. But Peter Grant had always managed the group with an iron fist, staying firm on certain fundamental principles. For example, Led Zeppelin never released a single and never appeared on television. Similarly, Grant took a dim view of playing at a festival among other groups, thus diluting the impact of his protégés' performance. "We were asked to do Woodstock and Atlantic [the group's record label] were very keen, and so was our U.S. promoter, Frank Barsalona. I said no,

because at Woodstock we'd have just been another band on the bill."

Instead, Led Zeppelin was in San Antonio, Texas, on August 15, then at Asbury Park, New Jersey, on August 16. The latter date is amusing on several counts: first of all, the gig took place about 135 miles from Bethel, so it was not far from the Woodstock festival. Furthermore, the first part featured another British musician, Joe Cocker, who headed to Bethel immediately afterward. Finally, a week later, Janis Joplin played at the same venue, an engagement set up by the same organizers. The spirit of Woodstock was therefore close by.

Led Zeppelin in December 1968, just a few months after the group got together. From left: John Paul Jones, Jimmy Page, Robert Plant, and John Bonham.

JEFF BECK

THE GROUP

Jeff Beck (guitar)
Rod Stewart (vocals)
Nicky Hopkins (keyboards)
Ron Wood (bass guitar)
Tony Newman (drums)

SETLIST

"All Shook Up" (Elvis Presley) /
"Morning Dew" (Bonnie Dobson) /
"Rice Pudding" / "Shapes of Things"
(The Yardbirds) / "Blues Deluxe" /
"I Ain't Superstitious" (Willie Dixon) /
"Jeff's Boogie" (The Yardbirds) /
"Jailhouse Rock" (Elvis Presley) /
"Around the Plynth" (Faces) /
"Beck's Bolero"

DISCOGRAPHY

In August 1969: **Truth** (1968) /
Beck-Ola (1969)

Several groups had decided not to go, but few had committed to going and then decided to cancel. Two, to be precise: Iron Butterfly, who reportedly demanded to be flown in by helicopter from New York, and the Jeff Beck Group, who are claimed to have canceled a few days before the festival.

Jeff Beck's cancellation in itself was not so surprising. The British guitarist was not known for having an easy-going personality. Following the release of their excellent second album, *Beck-Ola*, the Jeff Beck Group went on an American tour, starting on July 2. In hindsight, the lineup was to die for: as well as Jeff Beck, there were Ron Wood (later of The Rolling Stones) and Rod Stewart (a future solo superstar)—both from the group Faces—Tony Newman (the drummer who would also play with David Bowie, T. Rex, Eric Clapton, and many others), and Nicky Hopkins on piano. This dream team had time to perform 15 concerts on the East Coast before Beck caught a flight back to England, apparently without telling anyone else. The group's last gig was on August 1 in Chicago, exactly two weeks before the planned appearance at Woodstock. Nicky Hopkins was the only member of the group who would appear in the end, when he joined Jefferson Airplane on stage.

This was not necessarily regrettable. Given the poor organization of the festival, the maestro would likely have been annoyed, potentially sabotaging his own concert, and at worst refusing to go on stage.

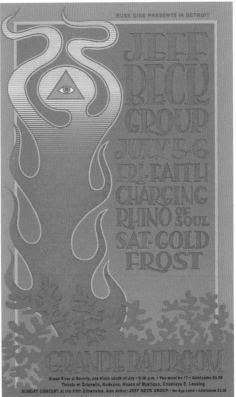

The epilogue to this story is more amusing. In 1999, Jeff Beck canceled, for the second time, his performance at Woodstock '99, two weeks after the bill had been officially announced, citing a clash of dates as his excuse.

Opposite: Jeff Beck, while in London, February 1969, was playing a Gibson Les Paul Standard sunburst at the time. This model of guitar would become associated with Jimmy Page, but not with Beck.

THE BEATLES

THE GROUP

John Lennon (vocals, guitar)
Paul McCartney (vocals, bass guitar)
George Harrison (vocals, guitar)
Ringo Starr (vocals, drums)
Billy Preston (keyboards)

Some groups had such an aura about them that their presence on the bill of a festival like Woodstock, huge as it was, would have radically changed the event's standing. The Beatles were not really willing to play live in 1969, but nevertheless initial negotiations took place.

In 1969, no artist had attained The Beatles' level of popularity. The four from Liverpool were seen as demigods around the world, their album sales were unprecedented, and they defined the conventions of the music world's star system, which have endured to this day. For all that, their relationship with live performance was not a simple one. First, their celebrity and the degree of fanaticism they provoked made their public appearances dangerous, whether because of the movement of crowds or because of the presence of unbalanced individuals. Second, the group had unceasingly developed its music, showing the way to everyone else in regards to experimenting with sound and making complex arrangements; however, the techniques for reproducing sound live at that time were nowhere near able to rise to the occasion. The clubs of Hamburg were a perfect setting for the steamy rock ambiance of the group's beginnings, but once it started to play in gigantic stadiums with sound systems that were not designed for music but for the spoken voice, the problems started. The gaps widened between albums that were increasingly more meticulously put together and short, botched live performances, for which it chose the simplest numbers in its repertoire. The Beatles played their last concert on August 29, 1966, at Candlestick Park, San Francisco, and never went on stage again.

Investigation

Billy Preston would no doubt have been invited to join the group had The Beatles played at Woodstock, and that performance would have been a good way of saying goodbye to the fans. Three theories have been suggested to explain the group's absence from Bethel. The first is that Lennon was in Canada at the time and the Nixon administration had no intention of making his entry into the country easy, given that he had been investigated for possession of drugs in England. The second theory is that Lennon was contacted by the organizers but made The Beatles' appearance conditional on him also playing with the Plastic Ono Band, and the organizers apparently declined. However, given the level of experimentation indulged in by some of the groups on the bill, this theory does not seem likely. Finally—both the least sexy but the most reasonable theory—is that the four musicians did not want to play live together again, were putting the finishing touches to what they saw as their last album (*Abbey Road*), and had already set their sights on their respective solo careers.

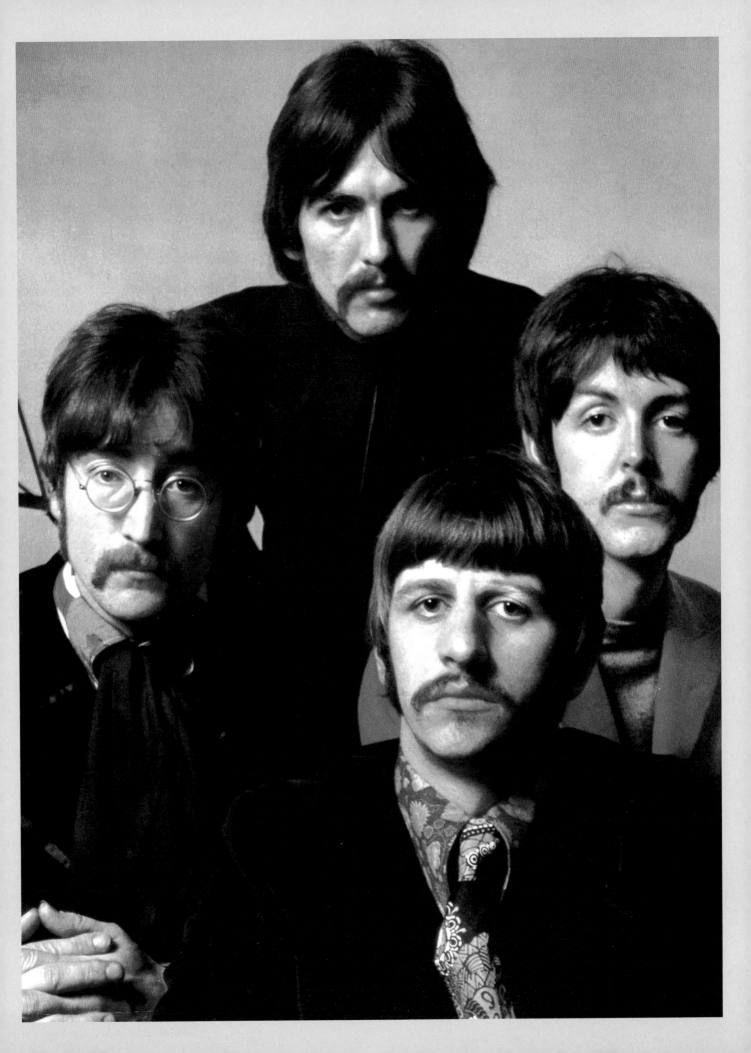

JONI MI

THE ARTIST

Joni Mitchell (vocals, guitar, piano)

THE SETLIST

"Chelsea Morning" / "Cactus Tree" / "Night in the City" / "For Free" / "Willy" / "The Fiddle and the Drum" / "Both Sides Now" / "Let's Get Together" (Dino Valenti) / "The Circle Game"

DISCOGRAPHY

In August 1969: *Songs To A Seagull* (1968) / *Clouds* (1969)

In a cruel irony of history, the artist who wrote the most beautiful song about Woodstock—which is heard over the closing credits of the movie and has become a symbol of the festival for an entire generation—could not be there to sing, because of a TV appearance.

The loveliest songs can come from a broken heart, and sometimes a missed rendezvous is enough. It was that terrible sense of a near miss with history that drove Joni Mitchell to write "Woodstock," the definitive song on the subject. And yet, she saw the festival by watching the television news in her manager's apartment in New York, and drew inspiration from the account given to her by Graham Nash, her partner at the time. In fact, two radically different versions of the song "Woodstock" were released simultaneously on Mitchell's *Ladies of the Canyon*, released in March 1970, and on *Déjà Vu* by Crosby, Stills, Nash & Young.

Invitation

What was the reason for this absence? Joni Mitchell would, after all, have fitted right in. The members of Crosby, Stills, Nash & Young were all close friends, and the fact that she played alone, accompanying herself on the guitar, would have made her a perfect addition to the mostly acoustic bill on the Friday. She had just released her second album, the superb *Clouds*, having become known through other artists singing her songs. Her presence at the festival, even on the album and in the movie of Woodstock, would have done her career a great deal of

good. Indeed, Mitchell was invited to the party, but her manager turned down the invitation.

David Geffen, who was also the manager of Crosby, Stills & Nash, had succeeded in getting his protégée onto The Dick Cavett Show on Tuesday, August 19. The show was a direct competitor to Johnny Carson's in the late night slot, and was watched by a young, hip audience. Shooting was scheduled for the afternoon of Monday, August 18—that is, the day after the end of the festival (or a few hours after the last gig, as it turned out)—and Geffen was worried that Mitchell would not be able to present herself at the studio in time to record the show, which is understandable given the monstrous traffic jams caused by the festival.

As if to make the point that Cavett was wrong, the other artists invited, Crosby, Stills and Nash, and Jefferson Airplane, traveled to the studio straight from Woodstock (Stills pointed out to the host his jeans, still covered with mud from the festival), illustrating that it was possible to make the journey in time. However, one important guest was missing: Jimi Hendrix had finished his gig at 11:00 a.m., so he was unable to get to the shoot; Geffen's fears were not completely unfounded.

In the end, the show was a joy to watch, and you could feel the atmosphere of the morning after a party shared by all the musicians who had been there. Joni Mitchell's performances were sublime. In "Chelsea Morning," she accompanied herself on the guitar, and in "Willy" and "For Free" on the piano. Finally, for "The Fiddle and the Drum," she sang completely unaccompanied, creating a moment of grace that took your breath away. In that moment, you could say that her missing the greatest festival in history had been worth it.

TCHELL

The history of rock was denied an incredible performance, as the biggest British group at the time was elsewhere for the weekend of Woodstock.

THE ROLLING STONES

THE GROUP

Mick Jagger (vocals)
Keith Richards (guitar)
Mick Taylor (guitar)
Bill Wyman (bass guitar)
Charlie Watts (drums)

SETLIST

"Jumpin' Jack Flash" / "Carol" (Chuck Berry) / "Sympathy for the Devil" / "Stray Cat Blues" / "Midnight Rambler" / "Under My Thumb" / "Prodigal Son" (Robert Wilkins) / "Love in Vain" (Robert Johnson) / "I'm Free" / "Little Queenie" (Chuck Berry) / "Gimme Shelter" / "(I Can't Get No) Satisfaction" / "Honky Tonk Women" / "Street Fighting Man"

DISCOGRAPHY

In August 1969: *The Rolling Stones* (1964) / *12 X 5* (1964) / *The Rolling Stones No. 2* (1965) / *Out of Our Heads* (1965) / *December's Children (and Everybody's)* (1965) / *Aftermath* (1966) / *Between the Buttons* (1967) / *Their Satanic Majesties Request* (1967) / *Beggars Banquet* (1968)

The Woodstock bill would have been radically different if it had included the Stones, but they were otherwise occupied.

Goodbye to Brian Jones

1969 was filled with problems for the Stones. The recording of the group's album *Beggars Banquet*, part of which was filmed by Jean-Luc Godard, became the soundtrack to the descent into hell of the founding guitarist, Brian Jones. He finally announced his departure from the group (evidently not through choice) on June 9. Less than a month later, on July 3, he was found dead in his swimming pool. Two days later, the Stones had scheduled a concert in Hyde Park, London, to introduce his replacement, Mick Taylor (formerly of John Mayall's Bluesbreakers) to the group's fans. The new member's first appearance thus became a tribute to his predecessor.

Absent for a movie

The change of guitarist might have been enough to put off the Stones from taking part in Woodstock. But the group was up to playing—as its fine performance in Hyde Park demonstrated—and the festival could have been an opportunity to introduce the newcomer to an American audience. However, the problem was a completely

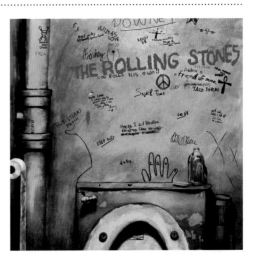

different one. Mick Jagger was in Australia for the shooting of the movie *Ned Kelly*, the biopic of an Australian outlaw. This was at a time when producers thought they could boost their movies' box office by taking advantage of a musician's celebrity (Lennon had already appeared in *How I Won the War* in 1967). The movie was a resounding flop, and neither Jagger nor its director, Tony Richardson, attended the premiere. The Stones would have been better off going to Bethel, but the group made up for it with an appearance on the American continent in November, starting in Colorado. The Stones also came up with the idea of holding a festival on the West Coast as an answer to Woodstock.

ABSENTEES ARE ALWAYS IN THE WRONG

Given the immense historic resonance of the Woodstock festival, it is tempting to imagine what the event would have been like if some of the absent groups had decided to join the party. Here are a few words of excuse for the most famous absentees.

Eric Clapton

The English bluesman was having trouble getting over the breakup of Cream and preferred to devote himself to his new group, Blind Faith, rehearsing intensively with his fellow musicians to avoid a repetition of their first concert, in Hyde Park on July 7, which had severely disappointed Clapton. The group split up in October.

Love

Arthur Lee, the Los Angeles king of psychedelia, was locked in an internal dispute within his group. He was therefore unable to respond favorably to the invitation.

The Byrds

This group, a founder of the psychedelic movement, were conspicuous by its absence. The musicians had decided not to take part, because they were worried that they would not be paid (an entirely justified fear, as it turned out) and thought it would be just another festival like many they had already taken part in. "[We] missed the best festival of all."

Jethro Tull

The group's flautist and singer, Ian Anderson, was not a fan of hippies and refused to take part in what he saw as a concert for naked, drugged people lying in a sea of mud.

Iron Butterfly

This proto-heavy metal group was scheduled to perform, but it seems the organizers decided not to go ahead. It is claimed that Iron Butterfly sent a telegram demanding to be collected by helicopter from New York, play as soon as they arrived, and be helicoptered straight back afterwards, but this report has never been verified.

Roy Rogers

The singing cowboy had been contacted with a request that he sing "Happy Trails," which featured in the closing credits of his television and radio show, to bring the festival to a close. Rogers knew his audience well and thus declined, fearing that he would be booed by thousands of hippies.

Chicago

The group was under contract to the promoter Bill Graham, who had scheduled appearances at the Fillmore West, San Francisco, from August 15 to 17, thereby making sure Chicago would not be at Woodstock—and thus making way for his protégés, Santana.

The Doors

The Los Angeles-based group was worried that Woodstock would be only a pale imitation of the Monterey Festival. Indeed, Woodstock's success was far better than expected.

Frank Zappa & The Mothers of Invention

Zappa was a true eccentric—being much more a freak than a hippie—and heartily detested the hippie movement, which he regarded as an excuse for taking drugs and not washing. He therefore turned down the organizers' invitation.

Good morning! What we have in mind is breakfast in bed for four hundred thousand.

Hugh Romney, a.k.a. Wavy Gravy

THE WORLD'S BIGGEST CAFETERIA

The extraordinary crowd that arrived to take part in the Woodstock festival presented a very practical problem. How should you feed what had become the third biggest city in New York state over the weekend?

Restaurant Associates, the company that handled catering for large events, such as sports games, refused to take on the task, because it was concerned by the number of festivalgoers and also because it doubted whether the estimates of numbers were reliable. Nathan's, the New York hot dog king, had been envisaged as the supplier, but it dissociated itself from the project when the festival venue was moved to Bethel.

LOVE—AND PROHIBITIVELY EXPENSIVE BURGERS

Charles Baxter, Jeffrey Joerger, and Lee Howard were finally given the task of finding a solution only two weeks before the first gig was scheduled. These three totally inexperienced restaurateurs formed the Food for Love company and immediately began to set up booths. The work was done in a rush, the number of hungry hippies was greatly underestimated, and long lines for buying food formed right from the start of the festival.

The restaurateurs had not planned for enough food, so the law of supply and demand came into force, inflating prices before people's eyes. It got to to the point that some angry festivalgoers burned down two booths on the Saturday night in protest. A hamburger then sold for a dollar—four times what it had cost at the outset.

Granola for all

Eventually, there was a great surge of solidarity to deal with the emergency. The residents of Bethel organized collections to get food to the hippies. The mothers of the Monticello Jewish Community Center, in particular, distinguished themselves, preparing thousands of sandwiches in record time.

Hugh Romney, head of the Hog Farm Collective hippie commune, which had been hired to take care of security, finally took matters in hand at the festival site on the Sunday morning, setting up booths that gave out free rice, vegetables, and granola. This blend of seeds and cereals was even distributed to the front rows of the audience, where people had not eaten for two days to avoid losing their place close to the stage. From then on, granola became the universal symbol of the hippie diet.

The brown acid that's circulating around us is not specifically too good. It's suggested that you do stay away from that. Of course, it's your own trip, so be my guest. But please be advised that there is a warning on that one, OK?

Chip Monck on stage, Saturday afternoon

THE HIPPIE DREAM

When Woodstock is mentioned, the image that comes to mind is a human tide of naked, drugged hippies. There is, of course, some truth to this image, but it is also far from epitomizing the experience of the festival, which was above all the gathering of a gigantic, peaceful community around the love of music.

It is impossible to know how much truth there is to such statistics, but it is generally accepted that 90 percent of the 500,000-strong audience smoked cannabis at some point or other during that weekend disconnected from time. Faced with such widespread use, the forces of law and order gave up, and no arrests were made for this reason.

The other star of Woodstock was LSD, the psychedelic drug par excellence, which was openly sold and distributed. For many, including certain artists, this was a way of getting the most out of the music, of abandoning oneself totally to the sensations rendered accessible by sounds. Heroin was also in circulation at the festival, and this hard drug was starting to have a devastating effect among musicians (The Beatles' *White Album*, for example, was supposedly connected to the discovery of heroin by Lennon). Cocaine, on the other hand, was not a hippie drug. It was present, of course, but its stimulant effect was not in tune with the movement's calm, relaxed philosophy.

Nudity and free love

Judging by photographs of the festival, one can easily imagine a Garden of Eden where Eve's outfit was de rigueur and clothes were banned as symbols of shame imposed on our bodies by Judeo-Christian society. This image has, in fact, been exaggerated to a great extent, and owes its longevity largely to the editing of the Woodstock movie, which gives prominence to naked breasts. It had not escaped the notice of the few photographers present that the lake behind the stage was a favorite place for nude bathing, which they saw as an opportunity for getting some fine shots. Although drugs and sex were part of the backdrop to the festival, they were not its central concern.

HAZY

A scene typical of the perfectly relaxed atmosphere at the Woodstock festival. Grace Slick, the Jefferson Airplane vocalist, sits next to a blonde woman holding a pipe in her hand. She is none other than Sally Mann, a well-known groupie on the San Francisco scene, who would later marry Spencer Dryden, Jefferson Airplane's drummer.

WOODSTOCK'S MICROCOSM SOCIETY

Despite the colossal scale the festival took on, those three days delivered what they promised and passed off truly in peace and with music. Nothing major happened that was regrettable, making Bethel a city with half a million inhabitants with a crime rate close to zero. For the last time, the hippie dream kept its promises at Woodstock.

Faced with the huge numbers of people arriving at the venue, and a lack of infrastructure, Governor of New York Nelson Rockefeller declared the festival site a disaster zone on the Saturday. And yet, violence had no place at the festival and, according to all the lucky participants, the festivalgoers were polite and friendly. Given the conditions they had to endure, this was certainly admirable.

Some cat's old lady just had a baby, a kid destined to be far out.

JOHN SEBASTIAN DURING HIS SET

Born in Woodstock

Many people born in August 1969 have claimed to have come into the world at Woodstock, but for most of them that is not true. It is difficult to verify—hippies were not fans of administrative procedures—but it appears that between two and four babies were born at the festival, including one in a car on the road to Bethel, and another in a nearby hospital. However, no supposed Woodstock Baby has proven his or her birthplace. The mystery remains unsolved.

Rest in peace

As with births, it is not so easy to come up with a figure for deaths at Woodstock. The accepted consensus is that two men died during the three days: one from a heroin overdose, and the other crushed by a tractor—the driver had not seen him, because he was covered in mud and lying on the ground asleep. Given the conditions, it is a miracle that no one else died. Torrential rain falling close to electrical equipment installed without proper safety measures could have had disastrous consequences.

THE GUITARS
OF WOODSTOCK

The festival began with Richie Havens' Guild acoustic, and ended with Jimi Hendrix's electrifying Stratocaster. In between those, the guitar was constantly showcased, in all its diversity and forms, to the point that it even found its way onto the poster and festival logo. The guitar industry was in the middle of an explosion at the time, with new designs coming and going—and this creative explosion was visible on stage. Here are seven guitars that made their mark at the festival in order of appearance.

Richie Havens' Guild

The acoustic guitar that had the honor of opening the proceedings was a symbol in itself. It was a Guild D-40, a guitar from a brand founded in 1952. It represented a new generation of instruments, less established and respected than Martins or Gibsons, however they were excellent pieces of equipment made in the United States.

To take the symbolism further (although it was probably unwittingly), Havens had chosen the D-40, which was a standard model that had none of the high-end refinement of the D-55, the flagship of the Guild range. At the time, a D-40 guitar would cost 280 dollars, while a D-55 would cost the tidy sum of 525 dollars; in today's money, it would be 1,900 dollars in comparison to 3,500 dollars. Democratic, without being cheap.

Santana's and Pete Townshend's SG Specials

By an amusing coincidence the 22-year-old Mexican kid who was making his debut on the giant stage, and the Briton, two years his senior, who had already trodden stages around the world for the past five years made the same choice. They both opted for the least refined Gibson SG, the Special model with two P90 pickups (Santana's was not as new as Townshend's).

For both musicians, the Special marked a phase of their career, and both would later move on to other models and brands. But this model would forever be associated with the intensity and liveliness of their 1969 sound.

Jerry Garcia's SG Standard

The Grateful Dead guitarist spent his life in search of a guitar sound. In doing so, he went through most of the classic models at some point or other of his career. In 1969, when the Dead had been in existence just four years, he had already played a Guild Starfire, a Les Paul Custom, a 1952 Les Paul Gold Top, and then another Les Paul Custom. For Woodstock, he played an SG Standard with a Bigsby vibrato tailpiece that appeared to be original.

It was easy to tell which of his guitars he had really liked, because he would adorn them with a sticker—a way for the musician to christen his conquest. The SG got an American flag next to the Bigsby tailpiece, so he must have liked it.

Johnny Winter's Electric XII

The Fender Electric XII was the 12-string electric guitar in the Californian company's range at the time. It was a commercial failure, which meant that in 1969 you could buy one for a derisory sum—which was probably what led Johnny Winter to buy his. He removed six of the strings to make it into a normal Fender with a highly original shape.

He kept it for playing slide guitar, because it was tuned to an open G tuning. This allowed for him to launch into "Leland Mississippi Blues" and "Mean Town Blues" without going out of tune in between.

Country Joe McDonald's Yamaha FG-150

The Yamaha FG-150 played at the start of the second day by Country Joe McDonald undoubtedly wins the prize for the cheapest guitar at the festival. This Japanese copy of a Martin Dreadnought, manufactured by a piano company that also made motorcycles, cost 99 dollars at the time—or about 670 dollars in today's money.

Yet Country Joe could also be seen at that time holding some fine Martin guitars. This was simply the guitar that happened to be lying about when the organizers pushed him on stage.

Leslie West's Les Paul Junior

Originally, Gibson had launched the Les Paul Junior in 1954 as a model for beginners who could not afford the Standard, let alone the luxurious Custom. But eager-eared guitarists eventually realized that this piece of mahogany adorned with its single P90 could sound superb if it was put into expert hands.

Leslie West totally made this model his own, and he made it desirable on the Woodstock stage, before Keith Richards and Johnny Thunders discovered its qualities.

Jimi Hendrix's Stratocaster

Jimi Hendrix had a strong preference for Fender Stratocasters, but he never fell in love with a particular instrument, switching from one to the other as the mood took him. Nevertheless, the white Strat he played at Woodstock has remained in the collective unconscious as the "Hendrix Strat" par excellence. From August 1969, whenever Hendrix is mentioned, it conjures up the image of his large-headstock Strat with its maple fretboard. Or an image of the guitar in flames, but that's another story.

ALTAMONT

The free concert held at Altamont on Saturday, December 6, 1969, was the yang to Woodstock's yin—its evil twin at the opposite end of the country. All the elements were there to make it a fine concert with a historic bill, however, everything turned out badly.

In fall 1969, The Rolling Stones embarked on their first American tour since summer 1966. The group was expected all the more eagerly, because this was also the first tour for Mick Taylor, its new guitarist. The tour was to end with a free concert in San Francisco, a proper celebration for the group before it returned to England. Altamont, a motorsports racetrack close to San Francisco, was billed as the West Coast's answer to Woodstock and, although the concert was to run for only one day, there were good reasons to believe this claim. It featured Santana, Jefferson Airplane, the Grateful Dead, and Crosby, Stills, Nash & Young, who had all been at Bethel, and, in addition, The Flying Burrito Brothers (the pioneer country rock group set up by Gram Parsons, formerly of The Byrds and a good friend of Keith Richards), and with The Rolling Stones topping the bill.

HELLS ANGELS

One of the glaring mistakes made by the organizers was to entrust the concert's security to the Hells Angels. This group of bikers, who are often associated with organized crime, were not known for their gentleness or tolerance, although their nonconformism rendered them compatible with the hippies. To make the cocktail even more explosive, these merry hell-raisers were paid in beer, as Sonny Barger, founder of the Angels' California chapter, related: "They told me if I could sit on the edge of

ON THE BILL

Santana
Jefferson Airplane
The Flying Burrito Brothers
Crosby, Stills, Nash & Young
Grateful Dead (who did not play)
The Rolling Stones

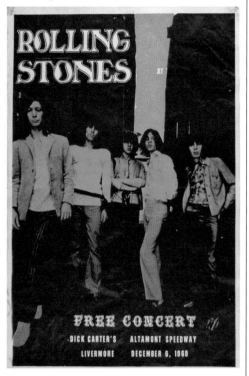

the stage so nobody could climb over me, I could drink beer until the show was over."

The combination of alcohol and the group's customary violence led to some unorthodox security methods. Notably, when an audience member accidentally knocked over one of their motorcycles, they apparently responded by beating him with pool sticks.

Meredith Hunter

Faced with the pervasive violence, Grateful Dead canceled their performance, and the audience had to wait patiently for nightfall. The Stones did not want to play beforehand, especially because Bill Wyman had arrived late. The Altamont concert degenerated past the point of no return during "Under My Thumb." Mick Jagger tried to soothe the audience by speaking to them calmly with his customary British charm: "Why are we fighting? Why are we fighting? We don't want to fight. Come on!" Keith Richards was more forceful: "We're splitting man, if those cats don't stop beatin' up everybody in sight. I want 'em out of the way, man." Nonetheless, something irrevocable happened. Meredith Hunter, an 18-year-old student wearing a conspicuous green outfit, approached the stage and was pushed back by the Hells Angels. He approached a second time and, when he was pushed back again, he pulled out a revolver from his pocket. One of the Hells Angels reacted immediately by plunging a knife into his back. Jagger asked for an ambulance, but it was too late. The group continued to play, and learned of Hunter's death on leaving the stage.

The 1960s died symbolically with Hunter. His murder symbolized the end of hippie ideals, rendered powerless in the face of violence as total and unjustifiable as that at the Altamont concert. What should have been a party became a nightmare, and nothing could ever be the same again.

WOODSTOCK THE MOVIE

Woodstock can legitimately be seen as the greatest musical film of all time, both because of its subject matter and treatment, and because of the way it was received by the public.

More than a simple record of the event, the movie made a big contribution to creating the legend of Woodstock for the millions of viewers who had not been able to attend and who thus experienced those "Three Days of Peace and Music" in movie theaters.

Michael Wadleigh, who until then had made only small-budget independent movies, took on the colossal task of filming the event, with financial support from the distributor Warner Bros., which doubtless did not expect it to be so successful. It would then take seven different editors (including Martin Scorsese, who was just starting his career) seven months to work through the enormous quantity of images made available to them, and *Woodstock* finally went on general release on March 26, 1970. The result was a movie lasting for more than three hours.

For certain artists, such as Santana, Ten Years After, and Sha Na Na, their appearance in the movie was a gigantic career boost. Their presence on the bill at the festival had certainly exposed them to a wide audience, but the transition to the big screen was on an incomparably greater scale. Overnight, they were offered tours and taking on venues they would never have imagined performing in just a few days earlier. The decision not to include certain groups was therefore a huge missed opportunity for up-and-coming artists, such as Johnny Winter and Mountain. Incidentally, those two groups would have given a harder image of Woodstock, and their omission tipped the musical balance in favor of folk and hippie psychedelia.

The 1960s are over

Woodstock was a turning point. The festival was both the culmination of the hippie spirit, thanks to the half-million people coexisting in perfect harmony, and the last occurrence of such a positive, innocent state of mind. The giants of hippie music, be it folk or psychedelic, were living their last moments of glory at Bethel, before a long spell in the wilderness for those who had not succeeded in reinventing themselves, whether they were Jefferson Airplane, Grateful Dead, or The Incredible String Band.

Many of the Woodstock idols would not survive long after their excesses. Canned Heat's Alan Wilson died on September 3, 1970, Jimi Hendrix on September 18 in the same year, and Janis Joplin on October 4. And that is without counting the groups that broke up without any tragedies, such as the The Paul Butterfield Blues Band in 1971, and Mountain, Creedence Clearwater Revival, and Jefferson Airplane in 1972.

Changing of the guard

The ambitious youngsters of the new school took over at Woodstock. Their approach was different in several respects. First of all, they put themselves forward more readily, right down to the name of their group, which might be their surname (Santana), their nickname (Mountain), or simply their name in its entirety, without bothering with a name for the accompanying musicians, which had been seen as the right thing in the 1960s. This change was more than just a way of presenting themselves; it marked the victory of the individual over the collective. Even if the name of a group bore no relation to its dominant member (for example, Led Zeppelin) individual performance was prioritized through extended solos.

The 1970s marked the start of the era of the virtuoso. A decibel arms race also began at this time between Iron Butterfly, Deep Purple, and a few others who pushed the equipment then available ever further in search of a thicker, heavier sound, thus inventing heavy metal. Part of this new paradigm was a change in the drug that was in vogue. Cocaine replaced cannabis and acid, accompanying a style of music that was faster, more urgent, and more aggressive.

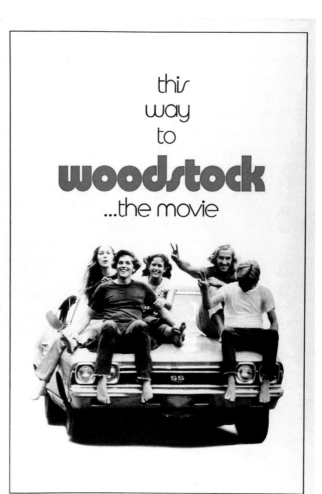

this
way
to
woodstock
...the movie

THE MOVIE THAT BROKE
ALL RECORDS

600,000 dollars

production cost

50 million dollars

takings in the United States, not including abroad

1 Academy Award

best documentary feature

2 Academy Award nominations

best film editing, best sound mixing

100%

score on Rotten Tomatoes

In 1996, the U.S. National Film Registry decided that the movie's cultural importance was such that it deserved to be included in the archives of the Library of Congress.

FEATURED PERFORMANCES	OMITTED PERFORMANCES
Crosby, Stills & Nash	Sweetwater
Canned Heat	Bert Sommer
Richie Havens	Tim Hardin
Joan Baez	Ravi Shankar
The Who	Melanie
Sha Na Na	Quill
Joe Cocker	Keef Hartley Band
Country Joe & The Fish	Mountain
Arlo Guthrie	Grateful Dead
Ten Years After	Creedence Clearwater Revival
Jefferson Airplane	*(they reportedly refused to appear*
John Sebastian	*in the movie, because they felt that*
Country Joe McDonald	*their performance had been poor)*
Santana	The Band
Sly & The Family Stone	Johnny Winter
Janis Joplin	Blood, Sweat & Tears
Jimi Hendrix	The Paul Butterfield Blues Band

THE
ALBUMS
OF WOODSTOCK

Today, when everything is documented exhaustively, it seems unimaginable that a complete audio recording of the Woodstock gigs still does not exist. Festivalgoers even had to wait four decades before they could hear extracts from certain performances again. Here, then, is an overview of the various releases of recordings from Woodstock.

Woodstock: Music from the Original Soundtrack and More

Released: May 11, 1970
Format: triple vinyl

The first record of Woodstock is described as the movie's soundtrack. Accordingly, it includes the same selection of artists: still no trace of Mountain, Creedence, or Johnny Winter, while John Sebastian, Crosby, Stills & Nash, and Hendrix are overrepresented. Regardless, the album does not completely mirror the music chosen for the movie, because it includes, for example, The Paul Butterfield Blues Band, who do not appear in the movie. The 21 tracks include 2 medleys of around 13 minutes apiece by Hendrix and Sly & The Family Stone. These are put together from different moments of the gigs in question—they are montages, not medleys that the artists actually played on stage at Woodstock. Some traces of the festival's special atmosphere were also added to the music for a more immersive experience. There is the sound of rain and the crowd's singing to stop it, a speech by Max Yasgur, and the announcement that the festival is free from that moment on. Also, the song "Sea of Madness" by Crosby, Stills, Nash & Young is taken from their September 19 concert at Fillmore East, New York, although they did perform the same number during their gig at Woodstock.

Burk Uzzle shot the photograph of the couple embracing at sunrise that adorns the album's sleeve. In 2009, journalists tracked down Bobbi Kelly and Nick Ercoline, who are still together 50 years after the festival.

Woodstock Two

Released: July 12, 1971
Format: double vinyle

Woodstock Two complemented the soundtrack, a year later, and consists of 16 songs, only one of which features in the movie: Jefferson Airplane's "Won't You Try/Saturday Afternoon." The album thus offered a good opportunity to hear unreleased numbers, and it was also the first appearance of Melanie and Mountain on a record made from the festival.

The Best of Woodstock

Released: June 21, 1994
Format: CD

On the occasion of the festival's 25th anniversary, Atlantic Records dug Woodstock out of its archives to produce several CD editions, starting with this "best of" that brings together 12 of the best-known songs played at the festival.

Woodstock: Three Days of Peace and Music

Released: August 9, 1994
Format: Boxed 4 CDs

This boxed set brings together the movie soundtrack, *Woodstock Two*, and several unreleased songs, thus finally including performances by Tim Hardin, Johnny Winter, The Band, and Creedence Clearwater Revival on a disk made from the festival.

Woodstock 40 Years On: Back to Yasgur's Farm

Released: August 11, 2009
Format: Boxed 6 CDs

This definitive boxed set marked the 40th anniversary and was put together by Rhino, a highly regarded record label that was careful to return as closely as possible to the spirit of the festival. The performances included on the six disks have not been enhanced, in contrast to what may have been done with previous releases, and the producer, Andy Zax, went back to the original recordings instead of reusing existing albums. All the artists present at the festival are represented, with the notable exceptions of The Band, Ten Years After, and the Keef Hartley Band. The last of these have never appeared on any official release, so it can be concluded that no satisfactory recording of their performance exists. As for the others, it can be assumed that there was a legal dispute between Rhino and those two groups.

Max Yasgur's speech is included in its entirety for the first time, as is the appearance of Abbie Hoffman during The Who's gig. Of all the Woodstock albums, this is probably the most immersive.

Woodstock Diary

Released: August 30, 1994
Format: CD

The last CD of the trio released for the 25th anniversary contains 14 songs, some of which were already included in the boxed set, as well as several unreleased performances, such as "I Shall Be Released" by Joe Cocker, "Love City" by Sly & The Family Stone, and "Southbound Train" by Mountain.

Live in Woodstock

Several of the festival's performances were released as independent disks. The first one was that of Ravi Shankar, who released *At the Woodstock Festival* in 1970—but one of the three numbers in his performance was replaced by a studio recording with added applause. *Jimi Hendrix: Woodstock* came out in 1994, but it contains only part of the performance. It was not until 1999 that *Live at Woodstock* included Hendrix's set in its entirety, with the exception of "Gypsy Woman/Aware of Love" and "Mastermind," the numbers sung by the rhythm guitarist Larry Lee. The year 2009 saw the highest number of releases of complete Woodstock gigs. Joe Cocker set the ball rolling, and he was followed by Santana, Janis Joplin, Sly & The Family Stone, Jefferson Airplane, and Johnny Winter. The last five's gigs were included in the 10-CD boxed set, *The Woodstock Experience*, which also included a 1969 studio album by each artist.

WOODSTOCK '94

'94

ARTISTS
WHO PERFORMED
IN 1969

Joe Cocker
Crosby, Stills & Nash
The Band (with members of Jefferson Airplane and Grateful Dead)
Country Joe McDonald
John Sebastian
Santana

THE
OTHER HEADLINE
ACTS

Bob Dylan
Nine Inch Nails
Metallica
Aerosmith
Red Hot Chili Peppers
Jimmy Cliff
Green Day
Peter Gabriel

Woodstock '94 was an attempt to rediscover the spirit of the original festival 25 years on, not far from the original site, and with some of the artists who had been there in 1969.

Indeed, the poster for the event directly referenced the original one, with two doves, and the acoustic guitar replaced by an electric one. "Three Days of Peace and Music" became "Two More Days of Peace and Music", because the festival was originally meant to run over two days, before the Friday concerts were added.

The public response was huge and the audience was even slightly bigger than at the original festival. In addition, various performances featured in this anniversary edition besides those that were simply celebratory. Bob Dylan sprang a surprise by agreeing to play a superb gig, despite being absent in 1969. The members of Red Hot Chili Peppers got themselves noticed by beginning their set disguised as giant lightbulbs and then all dressing up as Jimi Hendrix at Woodstock (with a white fringed jacket, Afro hairstyle, and red bandana). The set played by the Nine Inch Nails was also memorable for the fearsome appearance of the group's members, who were covered in dried mud.

Meanwhile, like Hendrix in 1969, Aerosmith's performance suffered from a slippage in the organization of time slots, and the group found itself playing at 3:00 a.m. on Sunday, in torrential rain, after the gigs of Nine Inch Nails and Metallica, as well as a fireworks display.

550,000
PEOPLE

WOODSTOCK

'99

Woodstock's third edition, Woodstock '99, was by all accounts an organizational disaster, and there was no Woodstock in 2009—a small gathering did take place, but nothing comparable.

From the beginning, no group that had taken part in the 1969 festival was on the bill, so the organizers clearly announced their intention of staging a huge, highly lucrative concert without bothering to celebrate the spirit of the original. In fact, the 1999 poster did not even allude to Arnold Skolnick's image. Jeff Beck was supposed to perform but canceled, as did Aerosmith, Sugar Ray, Foo Fighters, and the Smashing Pumpkins, doubtless sensing that the event would be badly planned.

The two stages were about 1¾ miles apart, it was forbidden to bring in your own food or beverages, the prices at the booths were crazy, and it was 100°F in the shade—and trees had been cut down to make room for the festivalgoers. Faced with these conditions, the audience became violent, burned down several booths, and fought among themselves. One festivalgoer died from his injuries. Faced with this foul atmosphere, MTV decided to break off its live coverage of the event and bring its crews home.

**ARTISTS
WHO PERFORMED
IN 1969**

John Entwistle
(The Who's bass player)
Mickey Hart
(Grateful Dead's drummer)

**THE
OTHER HEADLINE
ACTS**

Korn
The Chemical Brothers
Limp Bizkit
Alanis Morissette
Rage Against the Machine
Metallica
Megadeth
Red Hot Chili Peppers

400,000
PEOPLE

TAKING WOODSTOCK

THE IMPOSSIBLE FICTIONALIZED VERSION

Released in 2009 for the festival's 40th anniversary, the movie *Taking Woodstock* tells of the difficulties the organizers faced and paints a militant picture of the mood at the time. The movie has its strong points, but its lukewarm reception reveals a fundamental problem with its account of the festival.

The movie's budget was about 30 million dollars, but it only brought in slightly less than 10 million dollars. The figures speak for themselves: it was a flop. *Taking Woodstock* could have been a critical success while failing commercially, but that was not the case either.

Positive reviews were around 55 percent, which was far below those of the original 1970 documentary.

So, what does *Taking Woodstock* consist of? The idea of telling the story of the festival through the eyes of Elliot Tiber— a young man who introduced Michael Lang to Max Yasgur, and whose parents ran a decrepit motel in Bethel—was a good idea in itself. It was an alternative viewpoint that looked at the big picture anecdotally. The movie was an adaptation of the account written by Tiber himself, *Taking Woodstock: A True Story of a Riot, a Concert, and a Life*. The contents of this book have been debated at length by the other organizers, including Lang, who has claimed that he found Yasgur unaided. No account matches any other, and those who were there have not managed to agree as to what really happened.

The most interesting aspect of *Taking Woodstock* is the space given to the festival itself. Everything takes place all around and during those three days, but the protagonist does not venture too close to the stage. Woodstock is perceived through the hippies he meets and the drugs he takes, but the event itself is shown only through a psychedelic hallucination, a great ray of light with no stage or musicians visible.

This treatment clearly demonstrates the difficulty of telling the story of Woodstock through images other than in the form of a definitive documentary— which had already been done. That mystical, quasireligious experience cannot be fictionalized without being rendered trivial—which is exactly why, despite the scale of the event, no other movie has dared to do that to this day.

COACHELLA
WOODSTOCK IN MY MIND

What is left of Woodstock half a century on? In 2017, the singer Lana Del Rey wrote "Coachella—Woodstock in My Mind," one of few contemporary songs that refer explicitly to the festival of 1969.

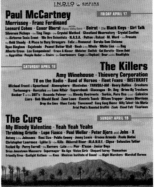

The first single to herald Lana Del Rey's fifth album, *Lust for Life* (which is another reference to the past, referring to Iggy Pop's 1977 album with the same title), is "Coachella—Woodstock in My Mind." It was released on May 15, 2017, and tells of the singer's experience at the Coachella Festival in California, where she was captivated by the performance of the singer Father John Misty. Del Ray describes the tension between this scene of sharing and peace, and the political climate.

The picture painted by Del Rey is fascinating for several reasons. First of all, it shows that Woodstock remains a powerful symbol of peace and love, as well as being the ideal music festival that is the yardstick by which all the others will be judged. Also, it clearly conveys the idea the younger generation has of the festival, with clichés such as garlands of flowers and long hair—a time so far removed that everything merges together (the refrain references "Stairway to Heaven," a song by Led Zeppelin that was released two years after Woodstock). Finally, she asks what

heritage Woodstock has bequeathed via festivals such as Coachella, a colossal event that runs over two weekends and attracts 250,000 people. Of course, entry is far from free, and sponsorship is rampant and omnipresent but, going beyond such cynicism (which could incidentally also apply to Woodstock), there is certainly something of 1969 about the idea of gathering away from the world and on the margins of society to listen to music.

INDEX

Page numbers in italics refer to captions.